ROGUE SHA̶̶̶̶̶̶ARE®

3 plays

PRETTY, WITTY NELL®

LOVE LABOURS WON

SWEET LOVE ADIEU
(Version II)

by

Ryan J-W Smith
BA Theatre Studies, MA Law (*Dist*)

(v. June 25, 2023)

Duckpaddle Publishing Ltd.

ROGUE SHAKESPEARE®
3 plays

© COPYRIGHT 1999-2023, Ryan J-W Smith

ISBN-13: 978-0-9515956-5-7   EAN: 9780951595657   First Edition

ROGUE SHAKESPEARE® 3 PLAYS first published in 2023 by Duckpaddle Publishing Ltd. *Pretty, Witty Nell®,* first published in 2023 in this edition by Duckpaddle Publishing Ltd. *Love Labours Won,* first published in 2015 by Duckpaddle Publishing Ltd. *Sweet Love Adieu,* original version first published in 2003 by Duckpaddle Publishing Ltd; *Sweet Love Adieu* version II first published in 2023 in this edition by Duckpaddle Publishing Ltd.

Front cover: Ryan J-W Smith as 'Sidney' in the world premiere of his *Sweet Love Adieu (v.2)* (photo by Annie Lesser). '*Love Labours Won* Players' artwork (p17) by Elizabeth E. Schuch ©2005. Reproduced by kind permission. Photo credits: p22, p43 Rich Clark; p44(bottom), p82, p86 (top) Ryan J-W Smith; p86 (bottom) Annie Lesser; p7, p44(top), p140 Matt Kamimura. Rogue Shakespeare®, *Pretty, Witty Nell®* and British Talent Agency® are registered trademarks of Ryan J-W Smith.

www.britishtalent.net

Duckpaddle Publishing Ltd.

www.ryanjwsmith.com   www.rogueshakespeare.com

Also available by

RYAN J-W SMITH

Sweet Love Adieu (original version)
ISBN-13: 978-0-9515956-2-6   EAN: 9780951595626
First published in 2003, Duckpaddle Publishing Ltd.

The Power Play
ISBN-13: 978-0-9515956-3-3   EAN: 9780951595633
First published in 2003, Duckpaddle Publishing Ltd.

Scan the QR codes or order via:

www.rogueshakespeare.com

www.ryanjwsmith.com

Also available by

RYAN J-W SMITH

500 SHAKESPEAREAN SONNETS
The Diary of a Poetic Quest for Truth

*"Candid, spiritual, philosophical and sometimes boldly political...
a landmark in literature"*
Watkins Magazine

*"Shakespeare managed to write 154 - Smith has penned more than three
times that number. ...splendidly contemporary... a tour de force"*
Herald Scotland

*"Impressively well-constructed... often startlingly expressive and insightful...
a fascinating and richly detailed picture of the author"*
Neon Literary Magazine

*"Shakespeare's record of 154 sonnets in his lifetime was breathtaking.
But what Ryan J-W Smith has achieved is simply awe-inspiring. Thought-
provoking, political, even hard-hitting at times, this collection of sonnets,
which took 4 years to write, is honest and very real. There is no layer to
scrape through - the reader is honoured with a very truthful portrayal of life,
which is beautifully crafted. Highly recommended"*
Book A Poet

*"Like reading someone's diary, their private thoughts and feelings captured
in verse... this collection shows a tremendous talent, and deserves to sit along
side your Poes, Plaths, and T.S Elliots."*
Mass Movement Magazine

*"Incredibly well written... a poetic achievement. A great gift for any
poetry lover in your life. Stunning stuff."*
Frost Magazine

*"An honest process of learning, healing and repentance...
a collection of inspirational, honest and didactic poetry"*
Mouth London

*"Masters of the Verse - Smith pays homage to the Bard with the
must-read collection of his own modern verse"*
London Planner

*"Truly brilliant... the best book of contemporary poetry
I have come across since the Four Quartets"*
Alan Jacobs, Author of '108 Sonnets for Awakening'

Available now in paperback:

500 Shakespearean Sonnets: The Diary of a Poetic Quest for Truth
ISBN-13: 978-0-9515956-4-0   EAN: 9780951595640
First published in 2012, Duckpaddle Publishing Ltd.

Example sonnet:

SONNET 484 - August 17th, 2011

You ask me how the world will change? I'll speak:
As people lose their jobs; their homes; their faith,
Our bankster-governments will break the meek:
In debt for good - you're worth more as your wraith.
The only massive increase? The austere.
The other place for growth, of course, is war:
You'll have to learn to kill, if you want beer;
Recruiters will take thousands of the poor.
As nations rise, and generals go berserk,
'Security' will kill our right to choose,
First where we are to travel - and then work;
'New Threats' appear: the ignorant confuse.
The iron-ring of commerce tightens fast;
The giant cull: the final word - be last.

Acknowledgements
Thank you very much!

Thank you to everybody who has had anything to do with my plays & sonnets over the years: actors; audiences; reviewers; festivals; sponsors; Arts Council England; venue managers; theatre companies, and absolutely everyone who is a part of the British Talent Agency® family - especially my amazing main assistants, Brenna, Gwen and Melissa. Special thanks to some of my biggest supporters, especially in reference to the plays herein. Namely:

My mother, for being there for me all these years; and my late father, who funded my early productions without hesitation. Love and thanks to both.

Bradley R. Bernstein, who has very kindly co-produced many of my plays including: the US premiere of *Love Labours Won* in 2015; the world premieres of *MacDeth!* and *Sweet Love Adieu (v.2)* in 2016, & the world/UK & NYC premieres of *Pretty, Witty Nell*® in 2019/2023. Thank you so much, Bradley.

Dr. Michael J Powers, KC for his constant support, encouragement, excellent advice, and kindness (and club lunches!). Thank you, very kindly, Michael.

My brother, who not only gave me excellent notes for the 2008 world premiere of my 4th play, *New World Order*, which received nothing but 4 and 5 star reviews, but who also directed an open-air summer park production of my 1st play, *Sweet Love Adieu (v.1)* in 2004. This production was special to me as it was the first time I'd ever seen one of my plays as just an audience member. I'll never forget what I saw…

Mid-way through the show, as the rain started pouring down, I looked around from under my large golf umbrella and expected the mostly uncovered and umbrella-less audience (all just sat on the grass) to quickly disappear and head for cover. Instead, something very strange happened - nobody moved. Every single person chose to stay, getting absolutely soaked to the bone, laughing at a new verse play by an unknown writer. I suddenly realised that I might be onto something: perhaps all these people weren't completely crazy - perhaps I should keep on writing in verse!? Thank you, brother (and Mother Nature) for giving me that moment. Clearly, it had an impact.

Chiefly, I thank Nature. The greatest gift I own is the ability to humbly place myself in service to Nature: aligning my plan to hers; listening, not demanding; feeling her love. I don't write - I listen gratefully, and obey.

ROGUE
SHAKESPEARE®

Ryan J-W Smith winning the Hollywood Fringe Festival International Award 2015
for his Love Labours Won, Hollywood, CA.

For all the fallen: injured, and the dead,
I will not stop - let truth and verse be wed.

Contents

pro bono publico

Author's Notes
by
Ryan J-W Smith, MA Law *(Dist)*

First, thank you for buying, or borrowing, or stealing my book! However you got hold of it, I'm very glad you are reading it. Thank you.

It's been suggested that I write a little something about each play to aid understanding of how/why each was written. Before I do that, please find some general notes for those involved in future productions of my plays.

Producers: I've given you a 50 minute tragicomic history; a 65 minute romantic comedy, and a very bawdy full-length (90 minute) farce. Use them wisely, and prolifically, as the need/desire arises (after you've paid for the rights, of course). N.B. Please do not hire inexperienced directors who make silly cuts and direct actors to perform my generally light-hearted comedies like heavy greek tragedies. Yes, this has really happened - more than once! Instead, please hire experienced directors of Shakespeare/verse comedies - ideally hire me, if I'm still alive and available. And yes, I may well be interested in directing your summer Shakespeare festival and/or your winter Rogue Shakespeare® festival!

Directors: please do not cut/rewrite anything without my permission. If you need lines adjusted for your audience, please just ask me. Thank you.

Audiences/readers: please laugh at the appropriate moments. I'll cue you.

Players: be word perfect! Learn your lines so you can do them triple speed while standing on one leg, juggling. Then, and only then, start acting. Use transitive verbs. Keep up the pace. Respect the meter - not too fast, not too slow. Pauses must be either in the text, or truly earned. Don't worry about 'character' - you are the character. Verse comedies require big, almost dance-like physicality, combined with confident, stylised acting. Be 'natural', not 'real'. Follow Anton Chekhov, Berkoff (watch *'Actor'*) and David Mamet (read *True and False)*; forget Stanislavsky/'the Method'. Learn clowning: use liberally on stage. Play! Don't shuffle around: use physical stillness to let the audience into your eyes/soul. Share! Direct 80-90% of your lines towards the audience to keep them engaged. Remember, the play is for the audience - it's not about you. Ok. That's it. Now get on stage and have fun!

Pretty, Witty Nell®

A one-woman tragicomic history in verse

AUTHOR'S NOTES: *Pretty, Witty Nell* is a one-woman tragicomic history in verse that tells the true story of Nell Gwynne (or 'Gwynn' or 'Gwyn').

What better way to celebrate the life of this absolutely amazing woman than by writing her a tribute in the style of theatre (rhyming iambic verse) that made her famous? And, given she was such a one-woman force of nature (a common prostitute/actress rising up the ranks until she was holding her own in the royal court as a permanent mistress of King Charles II, no less) it seems to me fitting that it is also a one-woman tour-de-force show. I'm biased, but having seen my play performed very well, I truly feel that it's a stunning showcase for any actress that can rise to the challenge.

> *"A standout solo show - perfect!"*
> Broadway World

I also wrote the play as a celebration of women on the stage - a new tradition that Nell's lover, King Charles II, brought over to England from his time in exile in Paris. Nell was one of the first ever actresses on the stage in England, and she was beloved by almost all who had the good fortune to see her, such as the diarist, Samuel Pepys.

I've had the good fortune to work with some brilliant and highly dedicated actresses in my time. Obvious examples: Melanie Johnson; Hannah Attfield. Indeed, one of the best ever productions of my *Love Labours Won* was with the fabulous all-female cast of our 2007 production at the Edinburgh Festival Fringe. Thank you once again, ladies - I owe you lunch. (As a tribute I've herein listed you in the cast list for *Love Labours Won*.)

I also love that *Pretty, Witty Nell*® is a tragedy, a comedy and a history. It's my first history play, but I believe all my facts are correct and in good order. As such I would love to see this show touring around (and studied in) schools, as well as more theatre venues. I think it could be a great bawdy-but-not-too-bawdy introduction to verse plays for the younger generations, that also educates them about 17th century history/drama: King Charles II; the Restoration; the plague; the great fire of London; Dryden; Pepys, etc.

Love Labours Won

A romantic comedy in two acts

AUTHOR'S NOTES: I wrote this play specifically as an ideal fringe-length (1 hour-ish) showcase of my writing style. I'm flattered to say it worked, and *Love Labours Won* has received a lot of lovely reviews over the years (thank you!) - especially at the Edinburgh Festival Fringe in 2006 and 2007. So I think it's best to leave it to three of those reviewers to give you an overview of the play.

"Shakespeare's relevance to contemporary life is often challenged by champions of modern theatre. With 'Love Labours Won', actor-playwright Ryan J-W Smith has written an outstanding modern play, in Shakespearean-style verse, which neatly addresses this concern and – quite frankly – blows it out of the water…'

'Love Labours Won' is undoubtedly the best Shakespearean comedy not written by Shakespeare. Relevant? This is unmissable."
Three Weeks

"This piece by director/writer Ryan J-W Smith garnered fantastic reviews and awards at last year's festival. It's back again this time with an all-female cast and I'm happy to report it's still excellent.

To describe it as a brand new Shakespeare play is to sell it short. True, Smith has done an astonishing job simply writing a play completely in rhyming iambic pentameter and making it lucid and entertaining. But it's the fact that he makes it feel so contemporary which is the real coup.

The plot is convoluted (deliberately) and is stock Shakespearean fare about star-crossed lovers and deceitful partners, and is driven by a series of soliloquies. For me it really takes off when the device of a play within a play is introduced (think Hamlet, Midsummer Night's Dream) and the pace really picks up. This is no silly romp, however, with serious points to make about the nature of love and deception.

There is one astonishing soliloquy half-way through which, without totally stepping out of the world of the play, manages to condemn utterly George Bush's hideous foreign policy and implicate the audience in the atrocities that are occurring all over the world. We are guilty because, though we may tut-tut about it all, we do nothing... This gear change in the piece and the resulting momentary discomfort in the auditorium are brilliantly pulled off by writer and actress alike, and worth the ticket price alone

Will Shakespeare, who must be dizzy with spinning in his grave every year when the Festival comes along, would thoroughly approve of this company's skill and vaulting ambition."

Broadway Baby

"Just as the bard himself is ever our contemporary, Love Labours Won addresses man's enduring dilemma of responsible monogamy versus free-spirited debauchery. "Can faithlessness in man be called a crime?" asks one of our protagonists, and as he unpicks his quandary we see some of the Globe's finest traditions replayed: strong, resourceful women, hoodwinked noblemen, gender-bending tomfoolery – this play has them all.

Smith, in daring "to chase the canon of the bard" shows himself as master of the iambic pentameter and rhyming verse. He cleverly matches Shakespeare at his own game with an engaging script that is faithful to its 16th-century muse but takes a dash of today's vernacular."

Hairline

I'm very grateful and flattered by these reviews, and many others just like them. I hope you agree they do a great job of describing the play - likely much better than I could do. So thank you, once again, kind reviewers.

I also appreciate the observation that I am writing modern plays, using classic forms, that honour the past while dealing with modern issues for a wide-range of audiences. Thus, it's universal: funny pastiche *and* critical thinking in verse. It's so humbling and fulfilling when Shakespeare-lovers and Shakespeare-haters both thank me for doing what I do. Verse is magic: writing poetry gave me inner peace. This play tells a little part of that journey. I now live to share my good fortune - to give that magic to you.

Sweet Love Adieu
(Version II)
A bawdy, saucy, filthy farce in five outrageous acts

AUTHOR'S NOTES: Ok, I'll need to give you some context on this play.

I penned the original version of *Sweet Love Adieu* while I was at Trinity College back in 1999. It was an original five act romantic comedy, based very loosely on Shakespeare's *Romeo and Juliet*. It was the first verse play I ever wrote, but evidently I'd found my niche, and reviewers seemed to like it. Here are 3 quotes from various productions of the original:

"Definitely Shakespeare for a modern audience"
UK Theatre Network

"Takes one of Shakespeare's greatest tragedies
and turns it into a hilarious comedy...unremitting excellence"
British Theatre Guide

"Farcical, bawdy, a treat! A great piece of entertainment"
Three Weeks

Incredibly flattering - thank you so much. However, it was the first ever review of the 2001 Rogue Shakespeare® world premiere production at the Roman Amphitheatre in St. Albans that likely sums it up perfectly:

"There IS culture – if you want it. Smith's play is derivative but is also quite daring. It takes a brave man to take on Shakespeare at his own game but Sweet Love Adieu succeeds thanks to its sizzling comic energy...

...his sweetly romantic play cracks along at a good pace with a fine script which borrows heavily from ye olde Englishe. But he wisely opts not to delve too far into some of the more archaic Elizabethan phraseology. While not sticking strictly to iambic pentameter, the dialogue is extremely adept with some very funny couplets peppering the script along with some great audience asides. ...highly accomplished... this play's a comic delight."
St. Albans Observer

So, while *Sweet Love Adieu* had received lots of lovely reviews and pleased a lot of audiences over the years, the truth of one line in the St. Albans Observer review started to rub me as I improved:

> *"While not sticking strictly to iambic pentameter..."*

It's true. My first two plays, *Sweet Love Adieu* and *The Power Play* were not in iambic - not at all! More like a modern rap than Elizabethan verse, the rhyme would appear *somewhere* along the way, but it could be halfway into a third line rather than at the end of a couplet; and the meter was frankly all over the place. Note: from my third play, *Love Labours Won,* onwards I vowed that the meter and rhyme should be perfect. That is to say that all my plays, bar the first two, are now (or should be!) in strict iambic pentameter (excepting the odd line or two for deliberate effect; or where I am quoting another author, e.g. the King's tribute in *Pretty, Witty Nell®*).

Now, don't get me wrong, I do still love the original *Sweet Love Adieu.* Despite the imperfection of the 'verse', it is a very lovable text. But after the success of my iambically-perfect *Love Labours Won,* and one-man *New World Order,* I really wanted to turn *Sweet Love Adieu* into perfect iambic.

Jump to 2015. I've just won the International Award at the Hollywood Fringe Festival with a revival of my *Love Labours Won.* I'm flush with Rogue Shakespeare success and wanting more! I decide it's time to rewrite *Sweet Love Adieu...* The result is here in this book: the story was condensed; some roles got cut or doubled-up; the bawdy jokes became very, very bawdy jokes, and the meter and rhyme were (I hope) perfected.

Thus, it is a completely new animal - the sweet little romantic comedy turned into an outrageous farce. Some may prefer the original; others will prefer version II. Naturally, I would suggest you read/see/study/perform both, and decide for yourself! 😜

3 plays

ROGUE SHAKESPEARE®

PRETTY, WITTY NELL®

Ryan J-W Smith

Written and directed by the multi award-winning verse playwright

Written entirely in rhyming iambic pentameter, a one-woman tragicomedy about Nell Gwynne, the famous actress/prostitute and mistress of the wild British monarch, King Charles II.

"a standout solo show - PERFECT!"
BROADWAY WORLD

NOMINATED
INTERNATIONAL
AWARD
Hollywood Fringe
2019

ROGUESHAKESPEARE.COM

Pretty, Witty Nell®

or

THE PROTESTANT WHORE

by

Ryan J-W Smith, MA Law (*Dist)*

A one-woman tragicomic history in verse

Based on version: APRIL 16, 2023

Ryan J-W Smith
C/o British Talent Agency
www.britishtalent.net
0208 123 9110

Pretty, Witty Nell®

or

THE PROTESTANT WHORE

Duckpaddle Publishing Ltd.
www.ryanjwsmith.com   www.rogueshakespeare.com

Pretty, Witty Nell®

- NOMINATED -
THE INTERNATIONAL AWARD
HOLLYWOOD FRINGE 2019

"A standout solo show… This solo show was perfect just as it was! What a wonderful and totally entertaining way to learn tidbits of behind-the-scenes British history! No need to change a thing - other than to give it more performances to entertain a much wider audience."
Broadway World

"There is something literally overwhelming about seeing iambic pentameter created anew, out of whole cloth. It's like having a momentary glimpse back into what Shakespeare's time might have been like. And Ryan J-W Smith has once again created a masterpiece of such a show, this time about Nell Gwynn. I was blown away…"
Erik Blair, LA Critic

"An astonishing performance and fascinating story. …once you are in her world she's a delightful guide to late 17th century English theatre, social classes, politics, and court intrigues. And as Nell tell stories about the people and events in her life, a vivid portrait emerges of the storyteller herself. Having immensely enjoyed Ryan J-W Smith's screwball comedies in previous years, I was unprepared for this smaller, quieter, one-woman gem, which is a delicious balance to the larger pieces. It is smart, funny, moving, and always entertaining."
Eric Cornwell, LA Critic

"British verse playwright, Ryan J-W Smith, applied his quixotic quill to Love Labours Won and MacDeth! in Fringes past and won LA over - to iambic pentameter! This year his ode to Nell Gwyn arrived…a solo show… she's getting standing ovations, and the audience leaves enchanted…"
Charles Ziarko, LA Critic

Melanie Johnson as Nell in the world premiere, Hollywood, CA, 2019.

Dramatis Personae - World Première

As first presented by Rogue Shakespeare® in the Broadwater Theatre, Main Stage, Hollywood Theatre Row, Hollywood, CA, on June 23rd, 2019.

Starring

Ms. Melanie Johnson

as

Eleanor 'Nell' Gwynne

Directed

by

Ryan J-W Smith

Scene: London, England.

ACT ONE

House lights up low. Low music. A bare stage, save for a chair with arms (the throne) upstage centre. On the back of the chair rests Charles Hart's jacket; beside the chair (upstage left) a gravestone cross. Downstage left is small, open trunk with Nell's props in. They include: a brandy bottle (water with tea), a Cromwell wig, a tartan shawl, a dagger, a crown, Buckhurst's wig, a book, Louise's fan, the Critic's satire (paper or scroll).

Nell is pre-set in the auditorium. She welcomes the audience in as they arrive, joking and having fun with them. She has a basket full of oranges on her arm which she tries to sell to audience members. Once the entire audience is in, she directs her opening lines to people on the front rows, but played for the entire auditorium. She speaks with a Cockney accent. She is playful, sexual, confident and fun. Music fades out as she begins.

> NELL. O, go on, darlin' – buy an orange, do!
> > *Pretending someone has offered to "squeeze her".*
> You want to "squeeze my peaches"?! You're too sweet!
> > *Giving some fruit to a man.*
> Here, take this juicy sample, love – take two;
> > *She addresses another man.*
> Come meet me after, sir – I'll be discreet!
> I'm only kidding, misses! *(aside)* That's his wife!
> I save my pippin for our noble King!
> *(Sexually)* One day he'll 'pluck' me – from this lowly strife,
> So I can kiss – and lick – his royal ring!
> > *She laughs. Then she picks on another man in the audience.*
> O 'ave a laugh, there mister – why so glum?

10
> You're in the theatre – all may yet end well!
> > *Teasing him sexually.*
> Perhaps you'll pay so I can suck your thumb?
> *(aside)* He's feeling better, darlings – I can tell!

She moves upstage and sets her orange basket down.
> Our play will start within a moment's breath:

House lights down.
> A tragicomedy: my life – and death!
> I, Eleanor, or Nell, a Gwynne by birth,
> In 1650, I begin my days;
> From hoi polloi – as common as the earth:
> What mighty changes come from little plays!
> The context of my coming into grace,

20
> Demands a little history – bear with,

Let's all together recreate this space,
That I, for but this moment more, may live.
Imagine, if you can, in England green,
With Shakespeare dead and buried, comes a curse:
The Puritans - the Killjoys, hard and mean,
Religious in extremis – it gets worse!
For they abhor the theatre, pubs and sport:
Yes, Cromwell's Model Army keeps us taut!
Our civil war pitched royals versus rules;
30   Against the King, the Parliament did stand.
And this was not your gentlemanly duels:
For nine long years they fought on English land!
In Scotland, Ireland and in Wales too,
The Roundheads sought to overthrow the King!
I marvel at the bloody things men do,
The misery and suffering they bring:
One hundred thousand English, maybe more,
Plus fifty thousand Scottish, died too young;
And God bless all the Irish in this war,
40   For half a million life escaped their lung.
And my sweet Charlie's father, Charles the First:
Take note of his mistreatment, if you durst.
By 1649, the King was done,
The Puritans claimed victory – they thought;
The end of rule divine was there begun,
For that, and for self-governance, they fought.
They charged the King with treason, took his head!
'Twas Cromwell signed the warrant for this act!
          She impersonates Cromwell.
"'Twas cruel but necessary!", Cromwell said.
50   'Twas regicide and murder - that's a fact!
This miser, Cromwell, held us long and low:
A bible-basher, eager to subdue,
Fanatical, like you could never know,
A pleasure-hating murderer – it's true!
Can you imagine childhood dull like mine?
A Sunday walk or swearing earned a fine!
From her trunk she pulls out a Cromwell Wig and puts it on, imitating him -
think Basil Fawlty from 'Fawlty Towers' having a breakdown.
      "One day in every month ye all shall fast!
All theatres hence devoid of plays and cast!
On holy days thou shalt not darn thy socks!
60   That boy is happy – put him in the stocks!

The civil war put me in charge – all right!?
I'm radical! I'm Christian! And I'm white!
No girl should dress in purple, pink or red:
That's it! I'm banning orange – you're all dead!"
She takes off the wig.
O what a life of drudgery, my dears,
A monochrome existence – bored to dust!
A tyrant that gave anxiousness new fears,
Yet Cromwell gave exception to men's lust!
She puts the wig down by her crotch.
One business that did better than the rest
70   Was prostitution – mother taught me well;
She raises the front of the wig up and down with a smile.
Our bawd house? Well, my mother's was the best!
She tosses the wig back into her trunk.
She loved her brandy more than she loved Nell!
She grabs a bottle of brandy from the trunk.
The bawd house – like a brothel – with a bar,
I serve the men strong water; hear them talk!
And as I age, with puberty not far,
They'd like to squeeze my melon on their fork!
My elder sister, Rose, she takes the trade,
Along with all the girls my mother bawds;
The rudiments of living are displayed,
She uses the bottle of brandy as a 'sword' phallus.
80   I note all men be servants to their swords.
Concurrent with my strife, our future King,
Charles Stuart; Charles the Second, Charlie dear!
She kneels and hides behind the bottle – pushing it aside as if it is the branch of a tree.
Is hiding in an oak tree! Lest he bring
Attention to himself from soldiers near.
For he is sought by Cromwell, for his head!
My clever Charlie 'cross the channel, fled.
She puts the bottle back and takes the crown from the trunk. She impersonates Charles - think, perhaps, Caesar from 'Life of Brian'.
"Before I could take passage, hear report,
For six long weeks the common man I played:
She hides the crown under her skirt.
Disguised, I walked or rode from port to port
90   To find a ship to France, or be betrayed.
Such hardships I endured – they taught me well,
They stripped all airs and graces from my mode;

She flicks her hair back with her hand, with great affectation.
      I vowed to love the people – Nell can tell!
      To love you all became my sacred code."
She takes out the crown and polishes it where her fingers just marked it.
      You have to understand, Charles was a man
      Who mused on England's bosom every day;
      For common girls, he did us all he can,
      This was his work; his mistress was his play!
      When Cromwell died, oh how we did rejoice:
100   The Restoration gave us back our voice!
She holds the crown aloft and carefully places on the seat of the throne.
      'Twas General Monk, all done with Cromwell's plots,
      'Twas Monk – the general – evened up the score;
On 'Edinburgh', she takes a tartan shawl from her trunk and wraps it around her waist like a kilt.
      From Edinburgh, as General to the Scots,
      He marched to London, Monk would take the floor.
She adopts a Scottish accent.
      "My mission was to clear the past of debt,
      So martial law, loose England would forget;
      To free a fettered parliament's rebirth,
      So that this King might walk his English earth."
She takes off the tartan kilt and uses it as 'chest of gold'.
      Unanimous the parliament accept,
110   They offer Charles the crown and chests of gold;
      All Kingdoms three rejoiced at this precept;
      Like giddy children grown men cry of old.
She playfully wipes fake tears off her face with the tartan kilt, then throws it back in her trunk.
      It really is a wonder – think on this:
      Without a drop of blood on either side,
      A playboy moved our world from hell to bliss;
      In history, sweet Charles should be our pride!
      For where would Merry England be today
      Without the Restoration of our King?
      With balance of a parliament to sway
120   The monarchy to order – quite a thing! P
      Forgiveness was the heart of this concord:
      A peace between religions, without fuss;
      An amnesty to all, from past discord,
      'The Breda Note' – our Charlie authored thus.
      We barely slept – such wonder in our head!
      Upon his birthday, Charles and London wed.

She puts on the crown and sits on the throne. She impersonates Charles.
      "I, Charles the Second, 1661,
      Restored unto the throne from exiled France!
      I brought with me high customs, how they shone;
130   An era of frivolity, and dance!"
She claps, as if summoning dancers. She imagines the dancers coming on.
      Although he had to balance with the Lords,
She takes off the crown and puts it on the cross to her left.
      And with the common house – with parliament,
      He gave us girls, a chance to tread the boards:
      A noble right for women, heaven sent!
      This act should not be overlooked, my friends,
      He changed my life, for that I give him thanks;
      But think upon the message Charlie sends
She stands and moves downstage dramatically.
      As women take their place in theatre's ranks.
      Until this time, a man would play our part;
140   This special King, he changed the fate of art!
      Before I speak on theatre, be amazed:
      The drama of establishment in life,
      For our new king had Cromwell's body raised,
She takes out Cromwell's wig by the top hair, and holds it up in disgust.
      And he would cut his head off with a knife!
She takes a prop dagger from her trunk and holds it in her other hand.
      Before he took his head, he had him tried,
      His unearthed, rotting body dragged to court!
      His regicide by none would be denied,
      Convicted him of treason, as they ought!
She puts the dagger pointing up under the hair – as if Cromwell's head is spiked on the dagger. As she speaks, she moves it from one side of her body to the other slowly – like an executioner slowly showing everyone what happens to traitors. She speaks, venomously.
      He hung his corpse, a symbol to us all,
150   For decades yet to come, it would there sit;
      In Westminster, above the giant hall!
      His head upon a massive spike was split!
Slight pause. She speaks, politely.
      Composed, refined and regal – our new king:
She flips the wig back into the trunk.
      As Shakespeare used to say
Flips the dagger in her hand.
                           - the play's the thing!
She tosses the dagger into the trunk.

I found the theatre door through Duncan's care,
My Mister Duncan was a merchantman.
Our 'interchange' was always just and fair,
He clothed me well – I soothed, like young girls can.
Two years or so we took a tavern room,
160   And rolled together, right by Drury Lane;
I watched the theatre growing in its womb:
A path for pretty girls to wealth obtain.
For prostitutes were common then as muck;
An actress – something fresh upon the stage.
'Twas newly seen – attractive men would pluck:
If you could play it right you'd have a wage!
Through Duncan, then, I entered wit's façade;
In time, I'd help him rise to Honour Guard.
Two theatres were allowed in London town:
170   The King's, in Drury Lane, a happy house;
And Duke of York's, with Betterton's renown,
But in the King's I find my future spouse.
Our playwrights, ripe with appetite, let loose,
Take full advantage, playing to the court;
They had no need to fear the hangman's noose:
Our comedies are made with King's support!
And Orange Moll, the mistress of us girls,
Instructed how to flatter and engage;
Adept at turning oysters into pearls,
180   I'd rise from Orange Seller, to the stage.
My banter with the pit would choke their throat:
Tom Killigrew, our manager took note.

She puts on Charles Hart's jacket.

Now fourteen years of age, under the wings
Of Charlie Hart,

She does a 'Charlie Hart' hair move and mocks him.

                  - "an actor with the troupe";
He taught me drama skills – and other things,
A method of advancement, to recoup.

She impersonates him - think any classic, over-acting, posh ac-tor, luvvie.

"I took her, like a father, schooled her hard
In acting, dancing, singing" *(as Nell)* – and the rest!

She impersonates him.

"I, Charlie Hart, my little Nell would guard:
190   Her tiny thighs exchanged for theatre's best!"
Inseparable, we loved offstage and on;
And I grew bolder, conning all with glee!

How quick upon my frame the spotlight shone.
The court and all gentility could see.
She moves over to her trunk, and kneels before it.
When first he viewed, his diary doth tell –
Sweet Samuel Pepys wrote, "Pretty, witty Nell."
She blows a kiss to an imaginary Pepys up in the gallery.
The plague then closed the city down from June,
She closes her trunk and takes it upstage right beside the throne.
We players move to Oxford with the court;
One hundred thousand people died too soon,
200   And that was just from London's grave report.
She steps forward.
When court returns in spring, it was not long,
She kneels down, her trunk in front of her.
Till London by a flame was done more wrong.
A third of all the city up in smoke -
Knelt behind her upright trunk, Nell acts sincerely like someone trapped in a building yelling out from a window ledge as they burn. These lines should be spoken slowly and truthfully.
"Fire! Fire! Our burning flesh doth cry!
We beg the fire service, London soak!
Please rain your water – do not let us die!"
A pause. She touches the throne beside her.
So fortunate I was for my charmed state,
As servant to the King within his charge,
Yet she that I became I did create:
She puts the trunk flat, and opens it.
210   I honed my skills from miniature to large.
When finally we're back at Drury Lane,
A sixteen year old Nelly starts her reign!
Nell wraps the tartan shawl around her shoulders.
Pepys loved my Lady Wealthy – my first lead,
Within The English Monsieur – what a part!
My reputation grows at lightening speed:
But I must pass this praise to Charlie Hart.
She takes off the shawl and impersonates Hart.
"In Dryden's tragicomic, 'Secret Love'
I, Celadon, a courtier, to bring
Nell's Florimel unto my wooing glove:
220   On-stage we are entwined by love and ring."
Poor Charlie Hart, I think he loved me true,
She takes off the jacket, kisses it, and hangs it on the side of the throne.
But soon, a Lord – then King – would Nell pursue!

We find I have a funny bone - or ten!
My jibing overacting suits this mode;
The how of fame's no question, only when,
The comedy of manners – my abode.
But theatre then, like op'ra is today,
Is not designed for common folk, you see.
More for the King and noblemen to play;
230   And Lord, they had their wicked way with me!
These poet-plays were conversations then,
Betwixt the brother's theatres – King's and Duke's;
The one would start a jest; we'd come again,
Our Howard or a Dryden would rebuke.
An inner joke, between the courtly crew,
And means for girls to turn our red blood blue!
In 'All Mistaken', or 'The Couple Mad',
I played the madcap lady, Mirida;
When chance gives us good fortune to be bad,
240   We mock our fellow actors, near and far.
Within the other theatre of the Duke,
She moves to the throne, puts on the crown, and sits.
King Charlie sits; his heart doth feel a pang,
She takes off the crown and puts it on the cross.
For in their play, which I would soon rebuke,
The small Miss Davis danced a jig – then sang:
She 'jigs' downstage; sinks to her knees, and mocks Ms. Davis, singing.
"My lodging on ground, my work is hard,
But what hurts most – the farness of my bard."
So taken with this actress was our King,
He raised her *(she stands)* to his royal bed - and more!
He placed upon her hand a precious ring,
250   And gifted her a house – the lucky whore!
Conspires I, with author of our play,
To mock our friends with comedy, most fine:
We thus adjust the ending, in a way,
To poke the eye of providence divine.
Within the plot of 'All Mistaken', I
Am chased by ardent lover, but he's fat!
So when he begs so sweetly, I deny;
Concluding our adventure, I sing flat:
She jigs again; sinks to her knees, and mocks Ms. Davis, singing (flat).
"My lodging on the ground, my work is hard,
260   But what hurts most – the fatness of thy lard!"
He rolls towards me - thus I roll away,

31

Around the stage we're rolling – see my leg!
Nell shows off one leg, revealing her bloomers.
Charles Sackville – that's Lord Buckhurst, saw this play,
And paid the theatre so my legs he'd spread!
Nell shows off both legs – stood in 2nd position in ballet.
I rolls myself to standing – he cannot.
Nell takes a dagger from her trunk.
I take a sword, embarrass him withal:
I mock that were he slim I'd be besot!
Nell uses the dagger as a phallus - up and then down.
And would that he were upright, he would fall!
So here the game, for theatres need their girls,
270   Seducing paying gallantry to view,
But actresses turn so to sell their curls:
Some Duke might buy them on their stage debut!
The playwrights of this era knew this well,
Their epilogues complaining to the wise;
The months they'd spend in training pretty Nell,
To have some noble rob them of their prize!
And like I said, Lord Buckhurst, bought me first:
She drops the dagger back into the trunk.
But time would tell, his ardour was rehearsed!
Nell bitterly takes out Buckhurst's wig. She puts it on & imitates him - think Boris Johnson.
"'Twas less a grand career – more like a shop.
280   A higher form of pimping, if you will;
The stage can halo beauty out of slop:
The highest bidder pays the trainer's bill!"
She takes off the wig.
So he, Lord Buckhurst, paid for me to leave,
So he could "poke around my teenage sleeve!"
She throws the wig back into her props box with disgust. She sits.
Lord Buckhurst bought me, down to Epsom we,
To make a merry house, his Lord and I.
Well, who could bar Lord Buckhurst? No, not me,
His breeding such, no actress could deny!
Admired for his patronage of art;
290   Enamoured both by women-folk, and men!
A virgin's thighs would offer up and part,
What chance for Orange Nell resisting, then?
He used me slow and soft, then fast and hard;
He even let his lackey have a go!
To coax me down, he played the wooing card,

She imitates Buckhurst.
     "But no-one craves what they already know."
     And 'gentlemen' soon tire of their games,
     So back to Drury Lane, used Nelly goes;
     There Charlie Hart now calls me vulgar names.
She suddenly spreads her legs and mimes Charlie Hart screaming the word
'Slut!' at her. She absorbs the abuse, lets it affect her, then speaks.
300   And forces me do tragedy – in prose!
     Lord Buckhurst taunts me, gives me nothing more,
     And though I be quite famous, Nell is poor.
     I hate the roles Hart gives me – so does Pepys;
     Our theatre loses audience these days.
     But do not think young Nelly sits and weeps,
She stands
     I know the swing of fortune, like these plays.
     And on that note, chastisement fills your host,
     For lazy actors thinking they work hard!
     These plays would run a week, or less, at most:
310   A repertoire from every rhyming bard!
     Our season from September through to June,
     With more than fifty plays upon our lips!
     No wonder girls like Mary Davis swoon,
     To take a break from witty rhyming quips!
     And when the King himself requests you cease?
     You do – and pray your belly may increase!
     It's funny how reality can top
     The height of artful drama in a fight!
     My lines, in Dryden's play - *I will not stop:*
320   *From knight, to lord, to duke, to greatest height!*
     And soon King Charlie's groin would target mine!
     The Black Prince play – the vessel. And my part -
     Alizia! A royal concubine.
     She woos the play's King Edward! Life and art!
     I charmed the king on stage, at seventeen:
     To half the world divine – to half obscene.
     He sent for me to visit. Thus, I did.
She moves to the throne and sits on it.
     A mistress of the King! A courtesan!
     His paramours were open. Nothing hid!
She picks up the crown from the cross and imitates him on "rampant".
330   'Twas normal for this "rampant, royal man!"
     Yet I did not directly leap to bed,
     For fear his losing interest, like the last.

So I would be a clever Nell instead.
She puts on the crown and impersonates the King.
 "I want to do you quickly – damn and blast!"
 I thus continued working on the stage,
She takes off the crown.
 While actress peers resigned for King's seed sown;
 They was the more endowed, the world could gauge,
She sets the crown back on the cross.
 But sometimes his liaisons I'd postpone!
 Though we was friends, they was my rivals too:
340 By every tactic Nell did Charles pursue!
 One day, in early 1668,
 I heard that Davis with the King would dine,
 So I invites her for a luncheon late,
She imagines Davis entering her lounge and sitting opposite her.
 To play a trick upon this concubine.
 My loyal friend, the playwright, Aphra Behn,
 From her great travels had a special root.
 This herb had enigmatic power then:
 The eater 'pon her shitter would take root!
She pretends to be stuck on her toilet with explosive diarrhoea!
 I feeds it to Miss Davis in some sweets;
She flips over the crown and offers Davis imaginary sweets inside.
350 The poor girl had the lot, I had no taste!
 'Twas odd, how to her home she quick retreats;
 "No dinner with the King? O, what a waste!
 Do take a little water, and some bread;
She offers Davis more sweets.
 Fear not, I'll entertain him in your stead!"
 Now don't forget, this monarch had a Queen,
 And she was most conservative and pure.
 It might be fair to say that she was mean,
 Since sex was his security, for sure!
 One night he had sent word he would to bed -
360 "Alone! Without the Queen!" For he was "sick!"
 Instead, I am received to tend his head:
 To bury him within – to stroke his… thick
 And curly hair of black – but, Charlie, hark!
 His wife arrives! Behind the drapes I spies:
She lifts up her skirt and hides her face behind it up to her eyes. She looks
either side then puts her chin over the skirt to speak.
 She sees he's well, but now 'tis not so dark!
 She spots a slipper on the floor, and sighs.

Nell drops her skirt and impersonates the Queen.
          "I will not stay for fear the harlot sold,
          That owns this thing might catch her death of cold!"
The Queen mimes tossing the slipper behind her. As Nell, she then ducks.
          And Charlie-boy would often visit mine -
370   On Newman's Row - what sweetness I recall!
          We'd play at house, much banter, cards and wine;
          My pigeon pie – a wonder for us all!
          Can you imagine, counter to this bliss,
She impersonates a French Messenger.
          When messengers from France's court do show?
          Down sewer streets they'd tip-toe.
          (in a French accent)   "Wat is ziss!?
          Ze King is wit zis trollop! Oh, no, no!"
Nell pulls a fake smile at the French messengers. She sits.
          That's why I loved sweet Charles, and he loved me!
          Unfettered by the rules of conducts past;
          An' most the nation loved us as we be,
380   For we threw off the shame of rank and caste.
          That said, the most I'd be was his best whore;
          But what would Nelly be should she want more?
          A year or two went quickly in this way;
          I still performed in theatre – well, why not?
          Then as I'm turning twenty, round that day,
          I births my son into his royal cot.
          That autumn, in my final play, I'm seen:
She stands, moving downstage dramatically.
          The Conquest of Granada – Dryden's quill.
          I take the part of Almahide, a Queen,
390   The rhyming prologue I remember still -
          But I shall not repeat it here today,
          For poets like *their* verse within *their* play!
She winks at the audience.
          O what a time it was, my loves – what joy;
          I pray you take my story to your heart!
          I beg ye ladies, be not low and coy,
          But should a King e'er hold you, never part!
          I gave him all – made him my husband true,
          Though in imagination's midnight charm,
She sits.
          Yet in the bedroom, we was fixed like glue:
400   I worshipped every minute in his arm.
          From Cromwell's strict observance, to such flare,

A restoration never better termed!
The naughty things we did I cannot share,
For piety today has been affirmed.
Yet it be false, for ye are worse that I:
You daren't admit the things I daren't deny!
She takes a book from her trunk.
Consider, also, clever Aphra Behn,
A Restoration playwright better none.
Some men forget, a woman held this pen!
410   For daughters could be poets, like the son!
A former spy for England 'gainst the Dutch,
As beautiful in mind as in her look.
Her words could be as carnal as her touch:
She flattered me too kindly, in her book!
"So excellent and perfect", calls me she,
"With charms, attractions, powers of your sex,
Eternal sweetness, youth and air." Aye, me!
She makes this simple courtesan complex!
"You glad the hearts of all with chance to view;
420   My shameful adoration, overdue."
She kisses the book and puts it back into her trunk. She is sat.
Now some of you may call sweet Nell a whore,
And let me here admit: I surely was!
But would you were in my shoes – born so poor:
To well-fed "why?", starvation shouts, "because!"
They say my dad in debtor's prison died:
Explaining all my gifts to pauper's door.
With equal weight I laughed as much as cried;
I kept my lowly place to raise the poor.
She stands.
For who would ransom kindness for themselves?
430   'T'would be a godless heathen, to be so!
I often took the chattel from my shelves,
And parcelled it that others love may know.
I count myself most lucky for my state:
She takes the crown from the cross and sets it on the seat of the throne.
If mine be good – King's charity was great.
I nudged him, often, guided from behind -
She stands behind the throne to one side and holds out her hand.
"To succour the most vulnerable and old!"
"For Chelsea Royal Hospital", I pined -
She stands behind the throne to the other side and holds out her hand.
"That all disabled soldiers cheat the cold."

I bargained plenty with my cheeky mouth!
She knees beside the throne to one side and holds out both hands.
440   "So that my children's children might enjoy."
He me bequeathed a house in Pall Mall south,
But that 'twas "merely *leasehold*!" did annoy.
I thus returned it to His Lordship's care,
Preferring "*Freehold* ownership!", I says.
He liked the jest – the error did repair,
Conveyed it to my name for all its days.
O Charlie! What a monarch ne'er forgot;
She touches the crown.
For only thee thy Nelly was besot!
She picks up the crown and sits on the throne.
The King and I, another night, I'll tell:
450   We find ourselves a tavern where we drink;
The Duke of York, his brother, there as well,
We drain a pretty bottle, as we clink.
But when it comes to pay the bill, these *men*,
So used to footmen carrying their purse,
They do not have the money! 'Scuse me then!
I pays the bill, and laughing, boldly curse:
"Od's fish! But here's the poorest company,
That I have ever got myself within!"
'Twas such comportment kennelled him to me:
460   I always could make Charlie Stuart grin!
She kisses the crown and sets it back on the cross.
Thank God no other ladies knew my gift:
(Aside) If you would keep him – make his spirits lift!
She stands, strikes a pose, and sings, politely at first, but ending vulgarly.
"Say can't you hear those sweet and dulcet tones
Of Nelly's common breath – and royal groans!"
But he, my liege, could never be just mine:
My birth was out the gutter – his divine!
My Charlie took another mistress soon:
Nell takes out a fan from her trunk – she holds the fan open in front of her chest when imitating Louise, and up to one side of her when talking to Louise – as if the fan is Louise beside her. Nell holds the fan to one side. Game: in unison, whenever Nell looks at Louise, 'Louise' (the fan) looks at Nell.
A noble girl, Louise, from Brittany.
This *little* French made English courtiers swoon,
470   The Duchess then of Portsmouth, she would be.
Nell imitates Louise, putting the fan in front of her chest.
"But zough I had ze title, and ze heir,

37

    Nell had ze people in her common hand;
    For she was one of zem – for Nell zey care,
    Zeir love for her and hate for me was grand!"
Nell holds the fan up to one side.
    King's other whores forgotten, but still paid,
    So we became the rivals – French and I;
    I mocked her every night that Charlie stayed,
    And how, within my lips, the king would die!
Nell imitates Louise, putting the fan in front of her chest.
    "I am ze lady – you a whore at play!"
Nell holds the fan up to one side.
480 Pray, would a *lady* let her partner stray?
    I chided her, "return to France, Madame,
    And take a husband worthy of thy rank!"
    Thank God the King had humour for my sham:
    For I – in front of her – he'd laughing, thank!
    I called her "Squintabella", for she had
    A droopiness about her least good eye.
Nell tilts the fan slightly to one side.
    A wanting actress, she would drive me mad:
    What waterworks on cue – she'd cry and cry!
Nell imitates Louise, putting the fan in front of her chest.
    "She dubbed me, 'Weeping Willow' – Charlie laugh,
490 His need for me – political, not vain;
    I'm here so Charles may bridge two warring path:
    So peace with France and England can remain.
    O pity me, for I had not Nell's wit,
    And she gave me no quarter – not a bit!"
Nell holds the fan up to one side.
    Yet she gave me such motive for my sword,
    Parading like a lady of the court!
    When any death from France we did record,
    She'd put herself in mourning – here's my sport:
    I puts myself in morning, just like her,
500 For someone – English – nowhere near my kin!
    The sides of her intent I loved to spur;
    To blunt my rival neatly on the chin!
Nell imitates Louise, putting the fan in front of her chest.
    "Oh, Charles, my distant cousin he is dead!"
Nell holds the fan up to one side.
    O, woe is me! Some Englishman did die!
Nell imitates Louise, putting the fan in front of her chest.
    "I need attention – naked – in your bed!"

Nell holds the fan up to one side.
 I'm so upset! Attend me! See me cry!
Nell pushes the fan closed with her free hand – as if to shut Louise up.
 Whatever she imagined, she got more:
She tosses the fan back into her trunk.
 A King's attention – plus an actor-whore!
 She never loved my Charlie, not like I,
510 For he was one of us – a common King;
 So I did all I could to her deny:
 An actor's skill in love can burn and sting!
 I took it on myself to play the fool:
 A licensed jester, honesty in puns.
 And in this way, all grandeur I did duel:
 To arrogance, my wit became my guns!
 I studied long and hard to plan my ruse,
 Each scene a mini play to act in court.
 It takes a lot of research to abuse;
520 To formulate the perfect, curt retort!
 But all these Ladies – mistresses, like I,
 Parading like their husband is the King!?
 They need the dose of truth that I supply:
 From off their cloud loud Nelly would them bring!
 If ye have traded gold for sex, be sure,
 You're not a noble Duchess – you're a whore!
She laughs and moves stage right.
 We had another son and called him James;
 To seek a title for my eldest child,
 In front of Charles, I beckons without names.
530 "Come here you little bastard son!" I riled!
 The King he remonstrates: "O!" So I toy,
 I have no better name to call him! Thus,
 He swift creates a peerage for the boy:
Nell imitates Charles knighting her son.
 "Now Baron and an Earl." *(Aside)* It pays to fuss!
 My place in court now notable to all:
 Unto my house King sends his Lords to call.
 To have good standing, all stay friends with Nell,
 For he with gross ambition, I can tell!
 I whisper in my Charlie's ear, beware:
540 You're safest in my bedroom, love – take care!
 Now I'll admit, I spent a pretty pound,
 I did enjoy the finer things in life:
She sits.

39

A carriage and sedan to bring me round;
No wooden spoons, but silver fork and knife!
Obscene amounts of silver made my bed:
A monument that Charles and I enjoyed!
And held I countless parties – guests well fed:
Full twenty full-time servants I employed.
But these were shows of luxury and health;
550   You have to wear the costume for the part!
And any man would tell, I shared my wealth:
To friend and foe, I'd portion from my heart.
I even let my first-born see Miss French:
No frost could truly dull this Orange Wench!
She takes a drink from her brandy bottle.
When mother died, they found her in a ditch,
Her brandy bottle blanket death did stitch;
But dead she was – so cold, and limp and still:
You cannot move at all when you're that ill!
I gave her rites, a princess would expect:
560   We Gwynne's were never coy, nor circumspect!
A wake – a long procession, full of joy,
To celebrate the life of Mrs Gwynne;
My friends at court, and theatre, joined the ploy,
From Lords to Duke, abolishing her sin.
From Coal Yard Alley, down to Drury Lane,
Then on through Covent Garden to the church;
Free beer to all and sundry, by my pain,
An answer to the mugs that did besmirch.
For do not think that all enjoyed my stay,
570   I quote a vengeful satire of the day:
She takes a scroll from her trunk and reads it.
"O Sacred Sir, protect this drab no more,
If you must have one use a handsome whore,
Of such foul hags there ne'er can be a dearth,
O send her to her dunghill mother – earth.
Old, wrinkled, ugly, loathsome as a grave,
She'd turn the stomach of your meanest slave."
She slowly tears up the scroll.
Endurance from experience doth calm
When evil critics wish us ill or harm.
It followed hard upon, in just a year,
580   My youngest boy, while studying abroad,
In Paris, James did die, of something queer;
That this was natural, I was not assured.

For poison was an awful, common thing,
And soon I would be pining for my King.
'Twas Sunday, all at Whitehall, as we did,
We had no care for worship, more for fun!
We minded not to keep our pleasures hid:
Both courtesan and gentleman undone!
The King was drunk with pleasure, as was I;
590   The Barons and the Earls did gamble hard;
Such dissoluteness none of us did spy:
Suspected murder – death had played his card.
At eight o'clock, on Monday morning sure,
The King with greatest agony did writhe!
His injury internal had no cure;
Until that Friday Charlie did survive.
His final words, upon your heart I carve,
Unto the Duke – "Let not poor Nelly starve!"

Slight pause.

Was ever there a King as kind as he?
600   So generous in dying, as in life!
The court, we fall to mourning, as I be,
His brother; all his courtesans, and wife.
I was denied to see the King by law;
I longed to hold his hand and bid farewell;
To give him from my heart my selfless core:
To say, "your soul with mine shall ever dwell."

She holds up the brandy bottle and pays tribute to the King.

"Here lies our sovereign lord the king
Whose word no man relies on;
Who never said a foolish thing,
610   *And never did a wise one.*
A merry monarch, scandalous and poor,
But he's the merry monarch I adore."

She drinks.

The irony of my prognostic tale:
A whore assumed to love men for their wealth,
Become, within the stable to this male,
The only mistress mourning for his health.
I did not love for gold – I loved the King!
Within a sea of falsehood, Island Nell,
A simple shore to walk, and play, and sing,
620   A rare and special palace – fools will tell.
For what is there of gallantry to last?
Beyond the gates of living – all must die;

      For King and beggar, life will travel fast:
      While pleasure, by the moment, doth supply.
      I grew to be incapable of guile:
      As honest as a newborn infant's smile.

Slight pause.

      I will not lie, King's passing left me poor
      For I, alone, was pensioned not for life,
      But for the King's short will, like common whore;
630   The others paid as if a widowed wife.
      In sooth, I had been outlawed for my debt!
      And since my king was dead, shops did not fear
      Send bailiffs, without pity or regret;
      Thank God his brother's promise was sincere.
      Now crowned, the Roman Catholic King James
      Did pay my debts and pension me most kind;
      He saved me from the mortgage broker's claims,
      And yet this turned an axe for him to grind.
      He wished my son turn Catholic, and I!
640   My final act – the whore did King deny.
      Perhaps it was his pressure, or my vice:
      A stroke soon left me paralysed in bed.
      My dying lasted months – a cruel device.
      I make my will; confess before I'm dead.
      The Queen, now dowager, did part relieve:
      She gave my son a pension of her own.
      'Tis something, when a wife will lend reprieve
      Unto a mistress, common to her throne!
      And me? I left good sums unto the poor,
650   Relieving debtors from the prison walls;
      To family, and servants, all the more,
      And those who differed in religious calls.

She slowly rises and moves downstage. She speaks very slowly.

      Illiterate, I signed my will, 'E. G.' -
      Reminding all, the pauper that I be.

She slowly performs a very deep curtsey.

Lights fade to black.

Melanie Johnson as Nell in the world premiere, Hollywood, CA, 2019.

Opposite page: Ryan J-W Smith, dedicating the award to his late father when collecting the Hollywood Fringe International Award 2015 for his Love Labours Won, at the Ricardo Montalbán Theatre, Hollywood, CA.

Love Labours Won

by

Ryan J-W Smith, MA Law (*Dist)*

A romantic comedy in two acts

© COPYRIGHT 2005-2023, Ryan J-W Smith

Based on V. 3.1

Ryan J-W Smith
C/o British Talent Agency
www.britishtalent.net
0208 123 9110

Opposite page: Jade Allen as Caesus, Emma Canalese as Annabelle, & Victoria Porter as Edmund in the critically-acclaimed all-female box office smash production of Love Labours Won, in the Gilded Balloon Debating Hall, Edinburgh Festival Fringe, 2007.

Love Labours Won

Duckpaddle Publishing Ltd.
www.ryanjwsmith.com   www.rogueshakespeare.com

Love Labours Won

- WINNER -
THE INTERNATIONAL AWARD
HOLLYWOOD FRINGE 2015

*"The best Shakespearean comedy not written by Shakespeare
- this is unmissable!"*
Three Weeks

*"some of the most delightful, well-written verse you are likely to hear. A very
enjoyable, warm-hearted, brilliantly acted, funny tale of love."*
UK Theatre Network

"A damned good romp"
British Theatre Guide

★ ★ ★ ★

"His writing is amazing… Smith is one to watch"
Fringe Review

★ ★ ★ ★

"A mesmerising work"
Hairline

★ ★ ★ ★

"Astonishing… excellent"
Broadway Baby

*"one of the most acclaimed plays ever
to come out of the Edinburgh Festival Fringe"*
Broadway World

- PICK OF THE FRINGE -
EDINBURGH FRINGE FESTIVAL 2006 & 2007

Dramatis Personae - World Première

As first presented by Rogue Shakespeare® at the Edinburgh Festival Fringe in the Gilded Balloon Debating Hall, August, 2006.

Valentine, Duke of Sussex West	Theo Herdman
Caesus*, Duke of Sussex East	Adam D Millard
Lady Katherine, beloved of Valentine	Emma Lo Bianco
Lady Julia, beloved of Caesus	Adele Cameron
Annabelle, a talented and beautiful actress	Tessa Nicholson
Edmund, her brother	Ryan J-W Smith
Edgar, his brother	Palle Nodeland
Chorus	Ryan J-W Smith

(*pronounced *"say-zouss"*)

Directed by Ryan J-W Smith.

And as presented by Rogue Shakespeare® at the Edinburgh Festival Fringe in the Gilded Balloon Debating Hall, August, 2007.

Valentine, Duke of Sussex West	Elizabeth Arends
Caesus*, Duke of Sussex East	Jade Allen
Lady Katherine, beloved of Valentine	Emily Lawrence
Lady Julia, beloved of Caesus	Clare Harlow
Annabelle, a talented and beautiful actress	Emma Canalese
Edmund, her brother	Victoria Porter
Edgar, his brother	Caitlin Shannon
Chorus	Victoria Porter

Directed by Ryan J-W Smith.

Scene: Sussex, England.

PROLOGUE

Enter Chorus.

CHORUS. I pray ye, welcome all to our sweet stage
Where chance provokes us tread with hot verdure;
Prove witness, thence, to each and every page
Contained herein as we to thee allure.
Though our love call may vex poor scholars' wits
Who lay false claim to breathless labours lost,
We needs must scribe, no matter whom it twits,
Lest we within ourselves aver the cost.
Sith opportunity doth us beguile
10 To dare to chase the canon of the Bard,
We should not cower then to those erstwhile;
Nor look at greatness passed and say, "too hard!"
So from another upstart English son,
We here present our own Love Labours Won.

Exeunt.

I.1   *Enter Valentine and Caesus.*

     CAESUS. Dissuade me not, my love-sick Valentine,
     Thy pickled heart is wanting flesh to brine;
     Hath no sweet sauce to aid thee sure surfeit
     This youthful vantage so with thee ill-met.
     Thy amorous intents will do thee harm!
     I pray, make better use of wit and charm
     To broach the bearded gates all men would take,
     Yet, taken once, to nature be not fake:
     Thou art a duke, possessed with juice and jewels
10   To dazzle, daze and dupe the ditzy fools!
     Commit no crime against our sex, brethren,
     (Using the audience) Have her at nine; her friend at half past ten!
     VALENTINE. Duke Caesus, now hear me and then be moved
     Unto the heart of even love itself,
     Where holy trust and faith needs not be proved
     And beauty's vessel bears the richest wealth.
     Thou wouldst me 'suade to love the world as one,
     Whose soul and body I cannot contain;
     'Tis better, then, enfixing but to one:
20   In her find peace, from other roads refrain.
     CAESUS. This wayward path shall yet lead thee to pain.
     Thou canst not love a woman, man - 'tis plain!
     The comfort that thou seek'st without's within:
     To self then look to let love labours win.
Caesus looks around the audience, impressed by his own logic.
     VALENTINE. How may a valentine be self sans love?
     I needs must then have substance in my view,
     And cherish her, as dove to sacred dove,
     Thus never could I bid sweet love, adieu.
     My Kate mine angel is, my heart, my all;
30   Without her, know, thy Valentine would fall!
     CAESUS. Thou fallen hast into this desperate need;
     Art Romeo, 'tis true; to death wilt speed?
     "Love lend me thus a dagger; Kate is sped,
     I die, and die, and die! Oh look, I'm dead!"
     Thou many times and oft hast loved and lost,
     How long till you again be tempest tossed?
     VALENTINE. The love that I bear Kate shall ne'er be broke:
     To dream 'pon her is like to sleep awoke!
     CAESUS. This love shall burn upon the dawn of time!
40   Release desire, in place belay thy lime;
     Entrap the beak and wings of all these doves,

The world is far too wide - have countless loves!
VALENTINE. Thou never shalt persuade.
CAESUS.   'Tis utmost clear.
VALENTINE. From love I am delayed.
CAESUS.   Aye, so I fear.
VALENTINE. I must unto my lady, there I'll rest.
CAESUS. Perhaps she rests with others? Nay, I jest!
VALENTINE. Pray, dost thou jealous grow?
CAESUS.   Of thee? Lord, no:
A foolish boy thou art - I pray thee, go!
VALENTINE. A foolish boy?! Give instance to your case.
50   CAESUS. Thou hast not time to wisdom here embrace,
You must to church, a eunuch in the choir:
Go worship her; throw fuel upon the fire!
VALENTINE. Thy Julia is what?
CAESUS.   She is but one.
VALENTINE. She is not then thy lady?
CAESUS.   Nay, I've none!
VALENTINE. Farewell, Caesus. I shall thee see anon!
CAESUS. Go temper self! O, Valentine, be gone!

Exit Valentine.

How man may lead his horse to water's lip
And though he drinks, his horse will die of thirst;
So I imbibe, as Valentine doth sip:
60   The self-inflicted wound of all is worst!
O Valentine, how I thy mind abjure:
A votary - a monk to fond desire!
Deceivéd thus, he can accept no cure:
He calls for truth then truth he calls a liar!
With aching hearts fools think that it is wise
To dupe themselves by false external mirth;
The inner kindness fellows most despise,
The calming of our mind - our peace on earth.
But conquer this, and dolor sure will cease:
70   All hopes and fears are enemies of peace.
Caesus is bemused by the source and depth of his own logic.
Enter Annabelle. She overacts, wonderfully.
ANNABELLE. Aye, me!
CAESUS. *(Aside)*   And yet, what beauty cometh near?
Withdraw thee, Caesus; we shall overhear.
Caesus hides.
ANNABELLE. Wherefore love I whereat I am not loved?
O, speaketh not his name, cast thoughts aside;

Transfixéd to his eyes I'll stay unloved:
To virtue and to honour thus confide.
   She feigns to leave, then suddenly continues.
And yet, though he would scorn me, I love on,
Bewishing that my need were not a crime,
For I would have him take me, full undone,
80 His mighty tower how I long to climb!
Yet, from the vantage of this soaring heart,
I fear that he respecteth our love not!
I must, for self respect, take leave and part;
Too much I basely muse upon this plot!
   She feigns to leave, then suddenly continues.
Yet what, perchance, could come to stir his sense;
Inclining his big presence to our arms?
Much like a wayward lamb, I'll leap his fence:
I cannot stop - so powerful his charms!
O that we to ourselves could be thus true:
90 My dear, Duke Caesus, I'm in love with you!
Caesus jumps up.
  CAESUS. *(Aside)* So super wise! With feature heavenly!
My genius - she recognises me!
Caesus realises he needs to hide again. He hides.
  ANNABELLE. I would he could peruse my hungry mind,
A more exacting love he could not find.
Had I one wish to here be granted true,
I'd plant, within his heart, a seedling new,
And through my daily care grow strong as oak!
O, answer hard and fast - make whole the broke!
Yet, Annabelle, be soft; make peace with air;
100 Come, speak thee now no more. We must repair.
      Exit Annabelle.
Caesus comes forward.
  CAESUS. By blackened beard of Zeus! What nymph was this
Kind chance and fortune thus did plant in view?
Delectable and fair! O new-seen bliss
That feeds and bloats my rising senses through!
How like a plague am I infected thus
By airborne sight and sample of her seed,
Immunity lies weeping, there - a puss;
Infection of her honey love - my mead!
I'd think this be a gull, but she is fair,
110 And I her know to be not of our troupe.
I must no more of Julia so care;

53

Too many crusts a meal maketh of soup!
Yet of my nature to entrap all hearts,
And spread my interest where it doth collude?
A prince must pause - divinity imparts,
Lest he upon preferment doth intrude!
Avaunt, foul pride! My solitude, adieu!
Ye hath no place within this sweeter scene:
I shall, for true love's sake, make fortune new;
120   Uproot desire to thus replant and preen.
Though I have oft, no longer I'll deceive:
I'll Annabelle love; and Julia - leave!
                                    Exit Caesus.

I.2   *Enter Julia and Katherine.*
      JULIA. Bespeak, good Kate, and pray thee grant my mean
Wherein I may to solace sooner seek;
I beg thee, be my muse, to grace nervine,
Where my unloving lover loves me meek.
KATHERINE. *(Piously)* Take peace, my gentle Julia, be thus,
And let thy nature sweet be nurtured so;
Though thy enraptured Caesus thee succuss,
Yet, doth he love thee, all but he this know.
JULIA. His love upon his lusting piece is caught:
10   He useth me, then laughs at conquest's sport!
KATHERINE. If thou forlorneth be, I pray thee, part,
Lest anger's venal thoughts corrupt thy head.
'Tis better cease than persecute thy heart:
A living mind of pain is better dead!
JULIA. His too hard love already hath me vexed
Transgressions to commit of ill-conceit,
So I am lost, within a soul perplexed;
I shall myself by mine own game defeat!
KATHERINE. O, Julia, what is't that thou hast done?
20   JULIA. Self-sacrifice to set myself undone!
Thou knowest well the rhyming theatre troupe
That showed midsummer's dreaming nightly dupe?
KATHERINE. I know them well, a truly merry horde,
(Aside) Though half their cast should never tread the board!
JULIA. Thou 'memberest, of course, the girl played Puck?
That girl that every fellow wants to -
KATHERINE.   - pluck?!
JULIA. Ay, even she! And her have I employed
To bait my loving Caesus in her net:
His changing mind, devotion so annoyed

30   I her engaged, a man-trap to lay set.
        I asked fair Annabelle, for such is she,
        Upon the next occasion that befalls
        To give pretended note to true decree
        That she of he his body much enthralls.
        And thence, my Caesus, he will her pursue -
        To she, even perfection must reply!
        Then as he woos her, I shall be there too,
        Admitting questions he cannot deny!
        And yet, I fear, I have misplaced mine aim
40   By bringing near my heart pure beauty's child:
        She may rebuke, respecting love o'er fame;
        As he loves her, so she is thus beguiled!
        Then what becomes of jaded Julia
        That, like a Rex, is destined to ill fate?
        She'll fall into dark melancholia:
        A desolate and life-deleting state!
              By now, Julia appears to be completely insane.
        Then aid me, Katherine, help me tame my mind
        That is by circumstance turned so unkind.
Enter Annabelle.
        KATHERINE. Here comes thy copesmate new. We'll speak anon.
              Exit Katherine.
50   ANNABELLE. My lady, I bring news - love labours won.
        JULIA. O, Annabelle! Didst thou too truly fake
        And thus ensnare my lover's head with lies
        So stuffed and loaded, by his heat to bake,
        That pleasing self, so highly he will prize?
        ANNABELLE. I did, my Lady, as requested play;
        I was consumed, ingested much today!
        JULIA. O wondrous joy! How happy I am now!
        (Aside) All sorrow gone, I truly disavow!
        ANNABELLE. Forgive me, madam, may I take my dues?
60   JULIA. My money, sure! *(Aside)* What more can someone lose?!
              Julia gives money to Annabelle.
        A bill, sweet mistress, for thy labour's love.
        (Aside) I hope you rot in hell! *(Praying)* Nay, rise above!
        ANNABELLE. Sweet Lady, thanks, I relished thy commission.
        I'll take my leave, with joy, and thy permission?
        JULIA. Aye, go! And listen, quit this city fast,
        This town is tough *(Aside)* and pretty girls don't last!
        ANNABELLE. Yet our sweet troupe is to perform tonight,
        A truly comic afternoon delight.

JULIA. What play is it that ye shall make anew?
70 ANNABELLE. A past'ral note they call 'Sweet Love Adieu'.
JULIA. Why not sweet love a Christian, I beseech?
ANNABELLE. *(Aside)* Alas, 'tis not my place to school or teach.
JULIA. Then let me keep thee from thy labour not:
(with difficulty) I thank thee for thy part within this plot.

          Exit Annabelle.

And thus with gratitude I deal my doom,
Belace the bitter rim of mine own glass;
Now idly care will happy few illume,
Whilst we below them choke a poisoned gasp!
How came her sphery angel eyes so bright
80 That earth and heaven both do her invite?
All souls who glance upon them do despair,
Whilst I? I am as ugly as a bear!
Repugnant farts have beauty more than I!
You laugh?! I hear the truth in your reply.
And see you titter still at my expense?
No matter; I'm accustomed to offence!
For japes and quips and Julia are one!
What ignorance did force me muse upon
Such foolish knavery as I have played?
90 Methinks this ugly duckling won't upgrade!
If so, my salty tears are all you'll see;
Think nought of it! 'Tis nothing! Let me be!
Here's but the cry of insufficiency:
A playwright's sour, poking joke - that's me!

          Exit Julia.

I.3 *Enter Valentine and Katherine.*
VALENTINE. My one true love, how I of thee have missed,
So much the heavens now becloud my sense!
Of everything but thee I can resist;
Against thy love no siege could lay defence.
But comely, like a passage to the sea,
So might thee taste the depth of my sweet plight,
I speed my aching heart from I to thee;
Capitulate to me, forestall thy flight.
In lieu thereof take comfort in our trust:
10 Let me thee love, till we be turned to dust!
KATHERINE. My poet duke hath much bewitched my heart,
Unclasped the love held deep within me there;
And yet, till we be wed, I thee must part,
Of honour, virtue, modesty to care.

VALENTINE. Then dost thou not believe that I thee love?
KATHERINE. I am of all things else most sure of this.
VALENTINE. So let us lie amongst the red foxglove.
KATHERINE. An we do lie, or stand, thou shalt but kiss.
    They kiss.
Forget me not, my love, when I am sped,
20   As I thee love alive, I shall in death.
So let immortal words infect thy head,
As thou doth then from thought, so sue thy breath.
Uncover truth to find our meaning here
And let all senses fold upon the skin.
'Tis love alone shall overcome our fear:
Elate thy mind to let sweet life begin.
I must now take my leave until tonight,
I pray thee, meet me hence to see this play.
Once more, my love, till we exchange in sight,
30   From thence to be together, come what may.
    They kiss.   *Exit Katherine.*
VALENTINE. Such wisdom that unclasps my very soul!
To be so chaste, content and true as she:
Unto life's stable she is now a foal;
As pure as her I pray that I might be.
Then close mine eyes and lay me down with peace -
Valentine sits.
    I swear her force of life is guiding mine!
Relinquish fear, and trepidation cease:
Valentine closes his eyes.
    I must un-blind the folds to see the sign.
Slight pause. Valentine opens his eyes, concerned.
    Yet, could I be, if she be not my wife?
He stands.
40   I must confess desire divides me through.
I love her so 'twould surely cost my life:
'Twixt God and Kate, I her choose over you!
So let me cherish that which I have found;
The world I'll summon, savour and confound!
          Exit Valentine.
I.4   *Enter Caesus.*
CAESUS. Desire thus leads me hither to collate
The heart of that I long for: Annabelle,
That I may of my need swift infiltrate
And spawn a shameless heaven here to dwell!
That she an actress is, I now have gleaned,

Performing in this theatre here tonight:
Though such a splendid debut ne'er was screened
As her avowal - how I shall requite!
Enter Edmund and Edgar, away from Caesus.
Ah-ha! Here comes me some of her sweet band;
10   I'll ask for her location, then her hand.
EDMUND. What say thee, Edgar, this may be the swain
Our sister, Annabelle, did speak of hence.
EDGAR. I pray it may that we might name our pain
To grant a meeting thus at his expense.
Find fault, Edmund, in ought that he might say;
I shall befriend and rich we'll grow today.
EDMUND. Aye, let us act a scene, our passions stir,
So that this evening's viewers may concur,
The best of their high praise should go to us
20   For bearing of our souls, as we shall thus!
Edmund and Edgar strike theatrical poses. They both overact, fabulously.
                    Caesus approaches.
CAESUS. How now, good sirs, I would a word with ye
About a certain lady I have met.
Thou both art true, tis utmost plain to see,
I pray ye, dost thou know of my coquet?
EDGAR. What be her name?
CAESUS.   The ample, Annabelle!
EDMUND. Thou lustful slave! I'll take thee thus to hell!
          Edmund attacks Caesus.
CAESUS. Good God Almighty! He's having a fit!
EDMUND. I'll tear thee limb from limb you piece of sh-
EDGAR.   - Hit
… not our friend, O Edmund, man so strong!
30   EDMUND. *(Demonstratively)*
Our sister he would bend and force his dong!
CAESUS. Thy sister? *(Aside)* Tits Magee!
                    (To Edgar) Upon thy grace
I fall, and beg thy favour for my love.
EDGAR. We should contented be to aid thy place
To our sweet sister's tiring room, above.
Thy name?
CAESUS. Is Caesus, Duke of Sussex - East.
EDGAR. And Edgar, I. This Edmund; sometime priest.
CAESUS. How grateful I would be to both her kin
If our *vrais coeurs* might meet, compete and win.
EDMUND. Thou ape-faced villain! Aye! Thou fevered dog!

40   I know thy sport and curse thy poisoned lung!
   Thou would'st bewitch us with this foreign fog;
   My hands shall teach thee yet an English tongue!
     Edmund pursues Caesus.
   CAESUS. O Lord! O my! Good God! O Lord, I say!
   O help me, sir, I pray, take him away!
   EDMUND. Thou coward! Cradle-boy!
   EDGAR.   Edmund, enough!
   (Aside to Edmund) Methinks the fool is taken by our bluff.
   (To Caesus) Kind sir, I pray a word apart with thee
   That we might of thy worthy fortune see.
   Alas, dear friend, our brother's out of sorts,
     Edmund acts out of sorts.
50   An will not let thee hence to seek thy belle.
   CAESUS. Perchance I could atone so he supports;
   What penance could I offer him, pray tell?
   EDGAR. There is one note he holds above all prayers.
   CAESUS. To fast? Repent? I'd don a shirt of hairs!
   EDGAR. Nay, nay, sweet sir, 'tis nothing quite so bold,
   To ease his mind but takes a sum of gold.
   Plain gold, 'tis true, 'tis all that he doth seek,
   But grant a piece and you may take a peek!
   CAESUS. Alas, I have no gold upon me, sir.
60   EDGAR. I'll let you speak with him, if you prefer?
     Caesus quickly offers up a purse full of cash.
   CAESUS. Perchance a cache of cash could change his mind?
     Edgar snatches the purse.
   EDGAR. No less than this I'd dare to chance to find.
     Edgar throws the purse to Edmund. Exit Edmund.
   CAESUS. Must he from all proportion take his part?
   For such a role it seems a handsome wage!
   EDGAR. I do but seek, with love, to aid thy heart;
   A smaller boon than this would swell his rage.
   CAESUS. 'Tis fair and true, thou art a gentleman.
   EDGAR. I am thy slave, an' do but what I can
   To minister to thee, a wiser soul,
70   *(Aside)* Who'd rather gain a loss than lose a hole!
Enter Edmund with Annabelle.
   Ah-ha! Here's now my brother with thy flame;
Edmund pushes Annabelle forward.
   We shall then take our leave and quit the game.
      Exit Edmund and Edgar.
   CAESUS. O, mistress sweet, I come to aid thy plight

So might thee play with conscience-free this night.
I know that thou doth love me plain and true,
By this expense I shall of thee value:
As Juliet in need of Romeo,
Thy soil shall swift betake my seed to sow;
As doth the shore to surge itself lay bare,
80   So of thy heart is mine exposed, to care.
Slight pause.

Nay, speak thee not, I am resolved and set
'Tis clear to see we are too well well-met!
So let me grant thy heaven and thy peace
And take of thee thy hand ne'er to release.
            Caesus takes her hand.
Annabelle looks out to the audience, bored and slightly disgusted.

O, what a happy couple we shall be!
So much in love, as much as you love me!
How lucky thou must feel? I'm such a prize!
I'll warrant thou can scarce believe thine eyes?!
To find the object of thy hot desire
90   Beholding thee belike - O, holy fire!
Caesus drops to his knees, dramatically.

Good God above, we thank thee for this sign,
From hence shall we abide thy soft design!`
Caesus rises.

So let us part with but a lover's kiss,
Of pure delight there is no more than this!
            Caesus tries to kiss her. She knees him in the balls.
(falsetto) O chastity! To fight against thy will,
Though thou adore, thy virtue holds thee still!
            Caesus approaches. Annabelle beats him to the floor.
(Aside) I never thought that such a girl could be,
(To Annabelle) Upon my life, I'll let thee marry me!
Annabelle looks out to the audience in disbelief.

Nay, nay, no words, I know you must prepare:
100   In honour of thy craft I shall repair
Myself from thee and let thee hence above;
Until, on stage we meet, farewell my love.
                        Exit Annabelle.

How speechless doth her honour leave my lips,
Whilst her discourse, how trippingly she trips!
What finer breaths and sighs could someone make?
Unto true love this angel is no fake!
Enter Valentine unseen by Caesus.

60

She loves me, sure, 'tis no uncertain truth.
For future's sake I shall not be uncouth,
But marry her I shall! She must be mine,
110   To bend and nibble; smell, arouse and dine!
VAL. How now! What's this? Have I misplaced my mind?
Do I but dream: is Caesus being kind,
That he now reconsiders of his lot,
In Julia, he sees just what he's got?
CAESUS. Too fast thou art and generous by far,
Though, thou aim true - *J'ai découvert une* star!
VALENTINE. In plainest speech, without thy gallantry,
What dost thou speak? Explain thyself to me.
CAESUS. The sweetest sight these eyes have ever seen
120   Is set to be my lover and my queen.
Her name is Annabelle, an actress she;
Within this play mine angel you shall see,
And our poetic spirits thus have climbed
To fall as one in unity entwined.
VALENTINE. O, Caesus, how inconstant is thy heart?
You now misconster perfidy for art!
Thy Julia with this you do much wrong.
O foulest tune! I pray amend thy song!
How wouldst thou be if she didst thee deceive
130   By lowest assignation? I believe
Thou wouldst forswear her soul to purgat'ry
If she of thee enact adultery.
So use compassion hence to change thy thought
And let desire by nature swift be taught.
Then see that all thy craving is but fear
Of that we wouldst not see, nor speak, nor hear.
I have of late much thought and now I see:
Whate'er we are afeared of, that must be.
CAESUS. I have no fear of being that I am.
140   I pray, did you not notice? I'm a man!
Go preach thy foolish folly to the earth
An let me live by merriment and mirth.
VALENTINE. Today's new joy will turn tomorrow's pain
If from thy ignorance thee not unchain.
Remember how thy Julia did seem
When thou didst first behold her? *"Like a dream!*
An angel of the heavens!", you did cry
And begged of her with thee that she should lie.
CAESUS. My Julia has ever jealous eyes.

VALENTINE. What vision else to see your faithless lies?
And now you crave another out of fear,
150   Perhaps that Julia is insincere,
Or that she may yet cuckold you in hate?
I pray, do not refuse or hesitate
To mark the truth I here do plainly see:
'Tis fear that drives the slaver whipping thee.
CAESUS. *(Aside)* There be some note of truth in that he speak,
And yet, I fear my soul and I too weak.
(To Valentine) Avaunt! I'll no more listen to your store:
If women be my custom, I'm a whore!
Enter Julia and Katherine, unseen by Caesus.
And yet, I have but one relief to sell,
160   I'll love not Julia, but Annabelle!
                Caesus sees Julia.
(Aside) O hell! *(To Julia)* Sweet angel! How I have thee sought!
These last few days, I swear, I've thought of nought
But thy sweet face to kiss and charm and squeeze!
I pray, where hast thou been, you little tease?
JULIA. Thou knowest well enough I've been at home!
Awaiting thy request I sat, alone,
Despairing at the fabric of my life,
That I would wish a villain make me wife!
CAESUS. I was to call on thee? O, Lord forbid!
170   Methought it was for thee to lift the lid
And send a messenger to call me there,
(suductively) Whereat I would thee cherish and lay bare.
JULIA. I send for thee? What art thou now, a king?!
(mocking) I do beseech thee, let me garlands bring,
Wherewith I'll kneel, and bow and scrape my nose
And with submission bite upon thy hose!
                Julia is down on all fours, she goes to bite Caesus' crotch.
                Caesus, facing front, holds her back with just his hand on
                her forehead.
CAESUS. O, Mistress Quickly, how I have mistook;
The death of me began with thy false look!
JULIA. *(Rising)* How like a churlish child to me thou seems!
180   CAESUS. At least, my dear, a child partakes in dreams!
JULIA. Thou foppish fool, I hate thee more and more!
CAESUS. A fool indeed for loving but a whore!
                Julia and Caesus commence a 'spitting war'.
                They continue until they are face to face!
VALENTINE. Enough, good friends, I pray be not so vain,

That which we most desire oft proves our pain.
So, set each other free and all shall pass!
CAESUS. *(To Valentine)* I'm letting go of nothing!
JULIA. *(To Valentine)* Kiss my arse!
   Caesus and Julia kiss, frantically.
Enter Edgar, Edmund and Annabelle. Annabelle wears a mask.
KATHERINE. Why look, here come the players to the stage!
   Caesus pushes Julia away.
Perchance 'tis meet we sit, and them engage?
Valentine and Katherine sit on one side of the stage; Caesus and Julia sit opposite.
   Edgar approaches.
EDGAR. Pray welcome ye, good friends, to this night's play,
Slight pause.
190   God's teeth, I knew this line the other day!
    Alas, I have not conned my text in time,
    I'll have to make it up and guess the rhyme!
    I am, William - like Romeo, that was;
    I love this girl called Anne, but I'm unhappy,
    Why? Because: Lord Edmund, who is hither,
      Edmund steps forward, acting.
    Has betook me of my heart, he's gone and
    Locked her up with plans to bed, the dirty fart!
JULIA. This is the silliest of plots I've heard.
EDGAR. O that I grant thee, Madame, 'tis absurd.
200   But who are we to question what is fake?
    Our scene is but the playwright's first mistake!
    So let us now at speed our fiction sell.
VALENTINE. Is all this in the play?
KATHERINE.   I cannot tell.
EDGAR. We join the plot as Edmund woos poor Anne,
    Or so he thinks, but truly, she's a man!
      Edgar momentarily thinks this is hysterical.
    For Anne hath rescued been by William's mate,
    Who's now dressed like a girl, *(Dons a wig)* to act as bait.
      Edgar retreats as Edmund comes forward.
EDMUND. I here present Lord Edmund; regal mugger.
    Though some would say I'm just a nasty bugger!
210   I've banished William from fair Anne, his love,
    So I can shove my hand right up her glove!
      Edgar comes forward as 'Anne'.
    Ah-ha! She comes, a sonnet sweet to hear,
    I pray, art thou in love with me, my dear?

EDGAR. *(Falsetto)* O big strong Lord, I might yet love thee true,
If thou couldst change thy tone and learn to woo!
EDMUND. An that I have, for I have penned a verse,
Edmund searches for the paper in his pockets - it's gone.
Which now I wish I had much more rehearsed,
For I have left the paper in my house!
In unison, Edmund and Edgar look at each other in panic.
They look back to the audience. They continue, improvising badly.
To speak its voice, I'd have thee for my spouse!
220   EDGAR. *(Falsetto)* O, that sounds mighty wonderful to me;
Tomorrow we shall wed and happy be!
EDMUND. Hurrah!
EDGAR.   Hurrah!
EDMUND.   Hurrah!
EDGAR.   Hurrah!
EDGAR and EDMUND. *(Holding hands)*   Hurrah!
EDMUND. Then till that time, night-night, a-nighty-night!
Pause.
EDGAR.   Quite!
CAESUS. I swear this is both tragedy and farce!
          Edgar removes his wig and gives it to Edmund.
          Edmund retreats, in disgrace.
EDGAR. *(To Caesus)* Forgive us, sir, rehearsal time was sparse.
Yet, now here comes a scene ye shall enjoy,
It's Anne, escaping - bearded, like a boy!
          Edgar retreats. Annabelle approaches, removing her mask.
          She wears a large fake moustache.
          Valentine and Caesus both stand.
VALENTINE. *(Aside)* Upon my very life, an angel she!
CAESUS. *(Aside)* Her feature, grace and soul enrapture me!
          Valentine and Caesus notice each other. Both sit.
          Annabelle performs, over-dramatically, demonstrating the
          actions described in each line.
230   ANNABELLE. Enfranchised from my captor, thus, we sped,
Like eager doves that fly their holding boughs,
Unto the Friar's church, where I had fed
My hungry soul upon my lover's vows.
But that, when I arrived, there was no sign
Of Will-i-am to take my hand and wed,
Instead the friar yawned and spake his line:
          Edgar approaches wearing a bald-cap.
EDGAR. He's not at home; now let me back to bed!
          Edgar retreats.

ANNABELLE. So, heaving up my heart, I hastened home
To save my man as he would now save me,
240   But once again cruel fate would not atone,
As Edmund waited there with villainy.
    Edmund approaches.
EDMUND. You cheeky girl, I've pricked your little plan:
You tried to get away; I wooed a man!
Now get thee back inside, till we are wed,
I'll see thee mine, or else I'll see thee dead!
    Edmund retreats, triumphantly.
ANNABELLE. So, under guard, once more, am I thus caught;
Forsaken, lost, betrayed, bereft and bought.
    Annabelle lies down. Edgar approaches.
VALENTINE. *(Aside)* Beshrew my heart, what devilry is this,
That I would give my soul for but one kiss?
250   KATHERINE. How now, my love, you do not like the play?
VALENTINE. *(Towards audience)* I don't see how it's relevant today!
KATHERINE. Pray, how can any act of love be old?
Methinks the verse germane, unique and bold.
These characters could yet be thee and I;
I hope that no-one dies for I may cry.
    Edgar approaches.
EDGAR. *(Dramatically)* Our final act is heavy for its part,
Be warned, it is not fit for faint of heart.
Take care, sweet ladies, of thy humour here
For we shall rend thy fancy into fear!
260   Poor Anne, is dead, her torments now at peace,
The pain she could not bare, so took release
From all her human suffering on earth;
She has no choice but now to seek rebirth!
Her kin, and all, grow quiet with this act,
And even gross Lord Edmund turns his back
    Edmund literally turns his back to the audience.
On infamy and makes a pledge to serve
Her spirit, as in life she did deserve.
I now retake the part of William,
Who's battle with himself is here become.
    Edgar overacts, wonderfully.
270   *(As 'William')* O hateful sight, what vision do I see?
Dear God, I ask of this alone from thee:
That I might here take one kiss of my wife,
In lieu thereof I offer thee my life!
I thank thee then, for nothing more than this,

I'll take my vow of death with but a kiss.
He moves to kiss Annabelle.
VALENTINE. Enough!
CAESUS.   No more!
VALENTINE.   This is too sad an end!
CAESUS. He'll have me yet in tears, heaven forfend!
EDGAR. My Lords and Ladies, all may yet be well.
He moves to kiss Annabelle, again.
VALENTINE. No more! No more of this, I do thee tell!
Caesus starts clapping, Valentine joins in.
280   CAESUS. 'Twas excellent, my friends, a merry piece!
VALENTINE. Alas, 'twas just too good, it had to cease!
CAESUS. Away, until we have this play's encore.
VALENTINE. Though not Sweet Love Adieu but something more
Of politics and power.
CAESUS.   Aye, of force!
VALENTINE. That one about the prince!
CAESUS.   Aye, aye, of course!
EDGAR. As you command. Sweet ladies; gentlemen.
Exit Edgar, Edmund and Annabelle.
JULIA. Methinks my lords are moved by love again?
VALENTINE. What means you?
CAESUS.   Aye, what song is it you sing?
JULIA. To see the truth, 'tis clear: the play's the thing.
290   KATHERINE. Come, come, you wept to hear this player's speech.
JULIA. Admit ye have a heart, we do beseech!
VALENTINE. Alas!
CAESUS.   'Tis true!
VALENTINE.   That was the very nub!
CAESUS. We are both weak and strong!
VALENTINE.   Aye, there's the rub!
CAESUS. No more of precious rhymes!
VALENTINE.   We cannot bare!
CAESUS. Unto our chambers, all!
VALENTINE.   Let us repair!
Valentine and Caesus stare at each other like rivals.
                                   Exit Caesus and Julia.
(To Katherine) I'll follow after thee, go on before.
Needs must I pay the players - they are poor.
They kiss.   *Exit Katherine.*
As one light of another light consumes,
Or as the sea by force takes o'er the shore,
300   So vision of this newer love illumes,

Against the which my present love seems poor.
Is it mine eyes, or other's eloquy,
Her sweeter heart, or bitter apathy
That reasons me to be thus reasonless?
And yet, she is perfection, nothing more;
Against her virgin truth, false Kate's a whore!
Fie, fie, ignoble tongue! I thee success,
Command thee hence to quell thy lusty fire:
If I 'gainst Kate, 'gainst self I do conspire!
310   But what of Caesus? He's declared his aim,
And boasts how Annabelle doth he requite.
Methinks a friend should marvel at his gain,
Not steal away his pudding for a bite!
And yet, he loves her ill for he is false
And plays upon another's set of dice.
To rob him quick and fast is my impulse,
How is't without a sound she doth entice?
We have not spoke a word and I am hers!
Perchance I should hot-footed seek her out
320   And tell her of my love 'afore it errs?
'Tis better die within than live without!
If I can conquer o'er desire, I must;
If not, in Annabelle I'll lay my trust.

Exit Valentine.

Enter Chorus.

        CHORUS. So, Valentine alone doth cogitate,
        Upon the higher heart of Annabelle,
        Whilst Katherine and Julia must wait
        For both their lovers them the truth to tell.
        Duke Caesus spends his days now wooing sweet
        The eyes and ears of she that he would tame,
        Though who can say what answer he may greet:
        Unwise is he who plays a player's game!
        For theatre folk have spent a lifetime's thought
10   Considering the ways of all our kind;
        'Tis foolish for a dealing fool to court
        An actress, for his impure heart she'll find.
        Then what shall here befall our courtly crew?
        All answers will unfold - begin act two!
                         Exeunt.

II.1 *Enter Katherine and Julia.*

JULIA. What say thee, Kate? T'hath been now three long days
Since last we saw our lovers, thee and I.
I know, by sure report, what Caesus stays:
He shouts his lust to Annabelle's fair eye.
For plainly hath she told me of his suit,
And how he visits hourly at her door!
KATHERINE. At least she tells thee plain and is not mute.
JULIA. For sure she lies and takes him like a whore!
KATHERINE. I would not think as low as this from she,

10 Who lives to serve her species on the stage.
'Tis oft forgot by those who'd never be,
An actor's life is hard with little wage.

Katherine and Julia glance at the audience in unison.

Yet, for a pittance and the sounds of joy,
To serve the wiser playwrights of their time,
They wrench themselves from deity to boy;
'Tis noble, pure and valiant, not a crime!
Should it be Valentine who did her woo,
I'd trust her with my love, and so should you!
JULIA. Too trusting angel! How I pity thee;

20 An actress and a courtesan are one!
But take thy seat backstage and ye shall see,
'Tis cut-price meat for every mother's son!
And of thy newly secret Valentine,
Is it not strange he leaves thee here apart,
To lock himself away whilst thee do pine
And dote upon the object of thy heart?
KATHERINE. He hath been sick and musing much of late.
JULIA. Though not upon thy face, nor of thy gait
As he was wont to, whence you came in view;

30 Alas, but he is he, and you are you.
KATHERINE. What means you by this inference, dear friend?
JULIA. I note but what I see, and there an end.
KATHERINE. And where's the end, dear heart, in what you see?
JULIA. That there is nothing spent 'twixt he and thee.
KATHERINE. "Is nothing spent?" Why there's a barren line!
I thank, but do assure thee, we are fine!
JULIA. As fine as vintage port that's never supped!
KATHERINE. Give o'er this turn afore it turns corrupt.
JULIA. I'll warrant that you shall not come undone;

40 Find peace; relax, it's just a bit of fun!
I'm certain that thy lover *is* in bed,

'Tis but with whom I cannot seem to thread!
KATHERINE. Thou ape-faced punk! Thou jealous infidel!
Aye, wouldst thou have me share thy fearful cell
And set my heaven down as low as thine?
Thy love is not worth half my Valentine!
JULIA. At least my lover's faults become a man!
He lies and cheats, but what is new in that?
I'd rather have him love a courtesan
50   Than hold me by a perjured caveat!
KATHERINE. How dare you treat me so! A sacred friend!
Our unity is done; this is the end!
JULIA. At last, I may be free of thy pure heart;
How oft have I so wished for us to part!
KATHERINE. Go sell thy face for nothing, still 'tis dear!
JULIA. How nice to have thy feet and arse so near!
KATHERINE. Thy lover is a dog and so art thou!
JULIA. I always hated you - you little cow!
KATHERINE. Thou straight salacious whore!
JULIA.   You haggard witch!
KATHERINE. Thou ugly jezebel!
60   JULIA.   You filthy bitch!
KATHERINE. Joithead!
JULIA.   Maggot-pie!
KATHERINE.   Loggerheader!
JULIA.   Clot!
KATHERINE. Boar-pig!
JULIA.   Popinjay!
KATHERINE.   Crusty codpiece!
JULIA. *(Confused)*   What?!
KATHERINE. Be gone! Go spend thy hateful words elsewhere;
This friendly sting no enemy would dare!
      Katherine begins to leave.
JULIA. *(Sincerely)* Yet hold thee, friend, 'tis Caesus I abhor,
His crime, though I didst instigate, cuts deep.
I beg of thy forgiveness, be not sore,
But let me make amends - nay, do not weep!
I did not mean the words I here did speak,
70   Thy lover Valentine is thine alone.
Have pity on a foolish mind so weak;
Give me thy arms, this argument postpone.
      They embrace.
KATHERINE. O, friend indeed!
JULIA.   My sister, as thou art!

KATHERINE. Twin sisters, true!
JULIA.   Nay, do not cry sweetheart!
KATHERINE. In truth, I weep for that you're certain right:
Methinks on Annabelle he too doth gaze!
JULIA. No matter, for we all shall meet tonight,
To see the player's second of their plays;
And there we may thus settle all our woe:
80   If men-folk would be free, why, let them go!
Come, let us part, and with compassion walk
To find a sweeter subject we may talk.
KATHERINE. I'll follow thee anon, go on ahead,
Tonight we'll see our future soon to be.
And think not that I harbour what you said;
Our lovers will choose her, or thee and me.
            They embrace.   *Exit Julia.*
O, Valentine, how can this be our path?
That such sweet love today now causes pain,
When yesterday it forced us but to laugh:
90   Is all our search for happiness in vain?
What is't about desire - that love, once won,
Turns all that we have gained to something lost:
For as new treasures claimed we stare upon,
To think of us without we fear the cost.
And yet, we lived without and were alive
Before we had the what we fixed upon:
This is then not to live, but to survive,
Lest we can freely lose love labours won.
Afore I break my mind, I'll rein my heart
100   And with a tearful smile bid thee adieu:
Farewell, my precious love, here we do part -
I wish you sweet success in all you do.
There's something selfish in this human love,
That holds us here beneath beset with woe;
Should we, sans fear, have faith we'd soar above
And feel for those mere mortals left below.
Slight pause.
Perchance I should with kindness aid his mind
By gracing him with that all men should know?
If through the playing of this play he find
110   Instruction for his heart, he'll thank me so.
I am resolved - divinity be mine:
I'll let him go, and love my Valentine.
                        Exit Katherine.

71

II.2　　*Enter Valentine.*
　　　　VALENTINE. I must unto myself be certain true,
　　　　To this above all else I have been taught;
　　　　I cannot leave to love, and yet I do:
　　　　Long love for Kate and Caesus is too short.
　　　　But by my loving them I hate myself,
　　　　To exile happiness within my grasp!
　　　　If I should by their pain regain my health,
　　　　Of our strong bonds forever I unclasp.
　　　　Then what is to be done? I cannot say,
10　　　For all is but a fever of desire.
　　　　Is it true love I seek, or do I play;
　　　　Can love be true when fearful needs conspire?
　　　　Be there some dread that drives us to be awed,
　　　　As I within Duke Caesus did detect,
　　　　Or is it but that man is perfect flawed,
　　　　An 'tis our nature to all friends infect?
　　　　O, wiser men than I, with long dispute,
　　　　Could never find an answer to this line;
　　　　Of all philosophy this is the root:
20　　　Can faithlessness in man be called a crime?
　　　　Some say there's but one path to find thy ease:
　　　　To nurture on thy nature with the earth,
　　　　And treat all moments as a transient tease,
　　　　So fearless shadows soothe our fearful mirth.
Slight pause.
　　　　The choice is plain, 'tis Annabelle or Kate;
　　　　The time comes hard upon, my time is now!
　　　　No more opinion, come, no more debate:
　　　　I'll turn my faith and break my lover's vow.
　　　　O, gentle Kate, I would not hurt thee so,
30　　　But chance that fate should call, then we must go!
　　　　　　　　　　　　　　　　　Exit Valentine.
II.3　　*Enter Caesus.*
　　　　CAESUS. This is the hour my mistress bade me call
　　　　To see her play, another sweet prelude.
　　　　Though she hath entertained me, come nightfall
　　　　She ushers me away - it's bloody rude!
　　　　Full three protracted days I now entice,
　　　　And yet she proffers nothing but discourse
　　　　On love, compassion, faith and being nice;
　　　　Of her salacity she me deforce!
　　　　Such virgin-like immodest modesty:

10 'Gainst her profession thus she doth transgress!
An actress that is chaste? Absurdity!
Their laxity is pure and nothing less!
Methinks, perchance, she knows of Julia
And that's the reason for her faultlessness,
Though of her sort 'tis most peculiar
To heed, with such unheedful heedfulness,
About the other loves her lover stores!
What business is it of a libertine
Where-else her equal dabbles out of doors?
20 The faithless cannot ask for faith so clean!
In sooth, I start to question of my choice;
Methinks that Valentine could yet be right!
Perchance I should hold strong to but one voice?
To brawl against myself is then the fight.
And yet, should I but taste of Annabelle
One kiss, or yet again, one secret blow,
'Twould be the highest, proudest citadel
That any warring King could overthrow!
My mind is set, she shall be mine tonight:
30 I'll cock and strut, till she my vein invite!

         Exit Caesus.

II.4 *Enter Edmund. He speaks with heavy sarcasm.*
EDMUND. I do beseech ye, masters, grant no wits
To ought that is bespoken by these tits!
We humble humans know that to be good
Is like to work for nought, since no one should:
It discontents our natural self-interest
To 'be as one'; in others time invest!
Nay, nay, dear friends, 'tis surely not the way,
Lest we turn artsy, generous or gay!
A stand must be here taken for our kin,
10 There's but one course to take on earth to win:
The key is cash, an' to be gained through fear;
Supremacy is next, that's plain and clear;
Desire, lust, pride, greed - all fair game to me,
Fast-tracked to which is fame or infamy!
An' fame for nought at all but for itself,
Of all sweet riches, there's the highest wealth!
There's nothing I like better than to see,
Inept and useless pure celebrity!
O what a wondrous marvel of our age!
20 In years to come they shall inscribe this page

Upon the tablets stone of future sense:
If such is true, God speed the recompense!
But God be praised, we have good leaders true,
That show us how to gut the good we do:
Through just crusades, enduring, we shall be
A hemisphere of racists, you and me!
What happy days! I pray ye, play your part:
Do absolutely nothing; stone your heart.
Think not upon the children that we kill,

30   The women raped or soldiers blood we spill,
It's all for peace and freedom, as they say,
So raise a glass - hip-hip, hip-hip-hurray!
> *Pause.*

O no, sweet sirs, now's not the time for peace,
Nor of kind words, there's terror to unleash!
In God's good name, and as God's name is love,
Let's drop, with love, our hatred from above.
> *Pause.*

Forgive me, sirs, for I have turned you numb;
I pray, be not so blind, so deaf - so dumb.

Enter Valentine with a single rose.

VALENTINE. How now, good sir, I would a word with thee!

40   EDMUND. You come to woo my sister, Annabelle,
And would this night enfranchise her, I see.
To grace your presence here, I could her tell,
Yet what, sweet sir, would I get in return?

VALENTINE. Perchance a bag of gold would serve the turn?
> *Valentine hands Edmund a bag of gold.*

EDMUND. I go, but for your honour, not for gain.

VALENTINE. Be gone, for I would have thee back again!
> *Exit Edmund.*

What shall these eyes behold few moments hence?
The paragon of all that men pursue;
Her vestal face will laugh at my defence,

50   An' she shall by a look my tongue subdue.
I must be sure, and stammer not with fright,
Though all I would have calm in me doth quake;
With but the thought of her within my sight,
Of everything I am, I gratulate.
She comes!

Enter Annabelle.

ANNABELLE. My Lord, once more you do ascend
To flatter and cajole with your true oath!

(Aside) And yet, 'tis not Duke Caesus, but his friend,
Alas, what could it be doth call them both?
   Valentine extends the rose.
Much thanks, kind sir, for this sweet sentiment,
60 The gift of which turns hawk to silent dove!
I take from it thy sense and am content
T'unfold its private passages of love,
Which I believe you would intend me here?
   Valentine nods.
Yet cannot speak a word, for 'tis sincere.
(Aside) 'Tis so, no louder tongue could speak so true!
   Annabelle takes the rose.
   She addresses Valentine loudly, as if he's deaf.
I'll take this, sir, and bid thee fond adieu!
      Exit Annabelle, in disbelief.
VALENTINE. O, heaven's mercy, bless me from my tongue!
Do I yet breathe? Have I no air, no lung?
'Tis so, I live, and yet came not a peep!
70 I've lost her then - the mountain was too steep.
She's way above my station, that's for sure,
Now of my doleful state there is no cure.
I'm out of love with one that cannot be,
And hard in love with her that won't love me!
My heaven was but here upon this spot,
Yet there stood hell, for I was too besot:
My airless throat remembered to forget
The passion that I bare, and now regret.
What mercy, cure, contenting remedy
80 Will save me hence? I need some therapy!
Enter Caesus, Julia and Katherine unseen by Valentine.
It cannot be good sense to be so bad
At courting gentle folk - I must be mad
To not have set my heart to ink by quill;
O, would I had the strength to speak my skill!
A curse upon her perfect entity!
By this cold shore I turn love's refugee:
There is no sense to loving any maid
When love doth by itself relent and fade.
Needs must I turn from seeking love's chagrin,
90 To serve the art of lust that lies within!
CAESUS. What's this, has tender Valentine turned sane,
That he doth voice against his loving name?
I pray, instruct what medicine you took,

So falling blind I may correct your look?
VALENTINE. Good Caesus, friends, you have no need of fear.
KAT. What was't that thou didst speak just now, my dear?
VALENTINE. 'Twas nothing, but a foolish player's text.
I came here swift that I – nay, look not vexed!
'Twas but a silly piece of verse I conned
100   Whilst from thy side I did in pain abscond!
         Pause.
Ye trust me not and doubt this to be true?
         All shake their heads.
I shall then here recite it unto you:
Valentine improvises a poem, badly.
      O, Kate, that is mine angel and my heart
      I pray that we may never, ever part.
      For thee I'd cross a really big river,
      Though getting wet, I swear, I'd not shiver
      For thy love's like a snugly mantle
      To keep us warm, not to dis-mantle!
      So let me covet thee with this:
110   A cuddle and a lovely kiss!
         Valentine moves to embrace Kate, she recoils.
KATHERINE. No more, my love, our time is near and pressed.
JULIA. Come, let us call the players from their rest,
So we might sit a while and take some ease
From all our hard-felt labour, if it please.
KAT. *(To Julia)* Sit here, sister, that we might look this way.
         Katherine and Julia sit together on one side;
         Valentine and Caesus sit together, opposite.
CAESUS. How now, good sirs, we'd have this play today!
Enter Edgar, Edmund, and Annabelle still bearing Valentine's rose.
EDGAR. Have peace, calm duke, there's ne'er a need to shout.
A player's skill takes art.
EDMUND.   *(Aside)* You stupid trout!
CAESUS. What sayest thou? Some line about a fish?
120   EDGAR. That thou art like a great white shark!
EDMUND.   *(Aside)* You wish!
CAESUS. How now? Again! Some insult spoken quick?
EDGAR. Yet not too quick for thee!
EDMUND.   *(Aside)* You pompous prick!
CAESUS. *(Rising)* I'll have this fellow yoked in public view!
EDMUND. Descend, my Lord, this ain't Sweet Love Adieu!
There'll be no Lordly ruling of my sport;
This is our Colosseum, not your court!

Caesus sits.

EDGAR. So, by your leave, we'll now enact our scene:
Pray, sharpen up your wits and ye may glean
A margin of enlightenment this day,
130   If thou take note of this, The Power Play.

Every time, upon hearing the phrase 'The Power Play', the 3 players   quickly
perform a silly, rehearsed dance motif in unison.

EDMUND. Afore we start our tragicomedy
We needs procure a player from the stalls.
EDGAR. His part entails Don Juan like infamy!
EDMUND. In other words, he needs to have some balls!
EDGAR. Come, come, good sirs, one actor there must be
Within yourselves, we do not jest with thee.
EDMUND. Fear not the verse, for all hath gone amiss,
'Tis but with our sweet sister you must kiss.

Valentine and Caesus both rise, instantly.

EDGAR. How now?
EDMUND.   What's this?
EDGAR.   Methinks we have a scene!
140   EDMUND. Display thy acting looks and we shall deem
Who is't that shall with us this night retell
Our second stab, and kiss fair Annabelle.
EDGAR. Stand thus, good sirs, and show the look of love!

Caesus and Valentine present 'love'.

EDMUND. 'Tis wondrous, sure; a heave unto a shove!
EDGAR. Now solo shall we test ye for this part.
EDMIND. 'Tis hard to be so cruel, but cruel is art!
EDGAR. I charge thee, sir, give me the face of death!

Caesus presents 'death'.

God bless you, sir, what teeth! What lovely breath!
EDMUND. And now, you sir, portray the face of fear!

Valentine presents 'fear'.

150   A winner here! So real! So sincere!
CAESUS. A winner? Nay, democracy ye flout!
There was no vote - I want a second bout!
EDMUND. Becalm thee, sir, we are the ruling class.
EDGAR. Thy friend won fair and square.
CAESUS.   This is a farce!
ANNABELLE. Perhaps just one more round shall then decide
Who is't that shall be mine, and I'll preside?
CAESUS. Agreed, sweet angel!
VALENTINE.   Come, another duel!
ANNABELLE. Approach the man who holds himself a fool.

> *Valentine approaches, Caesus sits.*
> Duke Caesus, thanks, 'tis clear you're not there yet.

160   *(To Valentine)* Advance, my lord, and take that you may get.
EDGAR. Come up! Come up, and join our faithful crew!
> *Valentine goes up.*
ANNABELLE. Another girl is needed - we're too few.
(To Katherine) Why, this sweet maid looks innocent and fair,
Enough to play his mistress, if she dare?
> *Katherine goes up.*
EDGAR. *(Quickly)* So, all is set - *we'll now enact our scene:*
Pray, sharpen up your wits and ye may glean
A margin of enlightenment this day,
If thou take note of this: The Power Play.
Our story sets itself, though none know why,

170   In Florence, that's in Sweden. Nay, I lie!
EDMUND. In Italy we find this lusting prince,
Called Valentino, who is so convinced
That love and being true causeth but pain,
He sleeps with all he can and feels no shame.
EDGAR. 'Till his good father, Rufus, who is I,
As King requests his son no more to lie
With common girls and royal courtesan,
But get himself a wife and be a man!
EDMUND. Of course, the prince refuses, as he would:

180   He sleeps with two at once, just as you should!
EDGAR. So, Rufus, that's the King, his father - me!
Demands that he be married, or not see -
Hang on, I think I've lost the plot again.
EDMUND. I told thee from that weed you should refrain!
> *Annabelle comes forward. During her speech she uses*
> *Edgar as 'the King', Valentine as 'Valentino', Katherine*
> *as 'mistress', herself as 'lover' and Edmund as*
> *'Grenaldo'.*
ANNABELLE. The King of Florence would his son see wed,
Securing thus his kingdom from within,
But Valentino, Prince, is still in bed,
With mistress; lover; boy, with vice and sin!
So threats of exile from the king they come -

190   EDGAR. Be married so or banished in three days!
ANNABELLE. But foolish kings dictate themselves undone:
His brother's lust for power set ablaze!
Grenaldo turns the nemesis to all.
EDMUND. Upon the throne of Florence I am fixed!

> *Edmund fires a plastic arrow towards Edgar. It misses*
> *Edgar by a mile. Irrespective, Edgar puts on an arrow-*
> *through-the-head and dies, terribly, and slowly.*

ANNABELLE. So one by one the kingdom starts to fall,
Till none can stand, nor none can come betwixt!
Unless our once reluctant hero, here,
Can overcome his masters: hope and fear.
EDGAR. *(Aside)* 'Tis so, although her meter was too flat!
EDMUND. *(Aside)* There's not much left to tell now after that!
ANNABELLE. Come, let us play the part where he doth woo
His sweet, Maria, I shall give the cue
When he should kiss me - it shall be his name.
EDGAR. Go to, then!
EDMUND.   As you please!
EDGAR.   You take the fame!

> *Edgar and Edmund retreat, bitterly. Annabelle and*
> *Katherine address Valentine from either side.*

ANNABELLE. In truth, my Lord, we see you suffer much:
A plague of thoughts abuse thy loving mind;
Desire much leaves thee longing for my touch,
Whilst anger at thyself turns thee unkind.
KATHERINE. And ignorance of all thy faults breeds fear,
Which in retreat you twist to conscience clear.
ANNABELLE. Behold this body that ye here confuse
As that which holds the nectar to your needs,
And know that should you win it, you would lose:
Addiction starves the eater as he feeds.
KATHERINE. No man may rule this world, nor should he aim,
For such a path leads blindly to despair!
But learn to tame thy mind and lay true claim
To all wrong-doing that thou caused or dare.
ANNABELLE. Take each step for itself and hold thy faith.
KATHERINE. Let go thy life and let all dreams subside.
ANNABELLE. Serve others as ye walk beside the wraith;
Be humble, know thy enemy is pride.
KATHERINE. When harmony and grace make thy heart true,
And you can love enough to let her go,
The troubles of this world won't trouble you,
As through enlightenment true love you'll know.
ANNABELLE. So kindness drink, as you would drink your wine,
And all the world is thine, Sir Valentine.

> *Annabelle gives Valentine back his rose.*
> *They curtsey to him.*

79

Pause.

EDGAR. Now is your cue, sir!
EDMUND.   Sir, your cue is passed!
EDGAR. But kiss the girl!
EDMUND. *(Aside)*   How long can one scene last?!
VALENTINE. Great men of wealth who spend unwisely cry,
Whilst beggars who are thrifty learn to fly.
I thank ye both, ye council to my heart.
To win my love within without alarm,
'Tis clear that from desire I must depart;
240   For sanctity of all, find peace and calm.
Since when obtained my suffering will cease
And with detached observance of this life,
From earthly needs and fears I'll claim release,
To end, without preferment, others' strife.
I own the greatest treasure man may hold!
I pray that all our kin may chance to see
That happiness cannot be bought nor sold:
As slaves to love and kindness, we are free.
And so, I take my leave, my path begun:
250   To scribe, within myself, love labours won.
                Valentine bows to Annabelle and Katherine.
                          Exit Valentine.
EDGAR. *(Aside)* Alas, 'tis not the ending I know well!
EDMUND. *(Aside)* But all is well that ends, so what the hell!
          Edgar and Edmund stand to address the audience.
EDGAR. Much thanks, kind sirs, there is no epilogue,
EDMUND. What needs the world another monologue!
                          Exit Edgar and Edmund.
          Katherine offers Annabelle a ring.
KATHERINE. Well played, kind lady, this is for thy pain.
ANNABELLE. To free another's mind is greater mean;
Yet, I accept, that we might play again,
So faithless man may trust to faith unseen.
KATHERINE. A noble cause, may I then join your few?
          Julia and Caesus are still sat.
JULIA. What do they speak?
260   CAESUS.   I haven't got a clue!
                          Exit Annabelle and Katherine.
          Julia and Caesus rise.
CAESUS. What think you then, sweet friend, should we so part
As Valentine and Katherine here have done,
Or should we grant ourselves another start,

To see how it may end, what we begun?
> *Julia strokes Caesus' face. She then slaps him, pulls him*
> *to her - they kiss, frantically.*

JULIA. Come, let us from this silly place be gone;
From hence thou shalt be mine, and mine e'erlong!

> *Exit Julia leading Caesus.*

EPILOGUE

Enter Chorus.

CHORUS. So quick our time hath passed, now all is sped;
We trust that it was better seen than read?
Alas, 'tis in the players we must trust,
For theatre is the mirror that we must
Behold ourselves within to see without
Our need of need itself, there's little doubt.
Forgive us if we preach to higher hearts,
'Tis for ourselves we bring to life these parts,
So might we never be where we have been:

10   Ye would not care to see the sights we've seen!
Too hard the fearful infant will become,
'Till he arise or see himself succumb.
So for your children, take our saga spun,
And hold it as thine own love labours won.

> *Exeunt.*

Above: Sweet Love Adieu open-air in Hoboken, NJ with NYC skyline.
Below: Gray Hawks as William and Courtney Wright as Anne in Wilmington, NC.

Sweet Love Adieu

(Version II)

by

Ryan J-W Smith, MA Law (*Dist*)

A bawdy, saucy, filthy farce in five outrageous acts

Based on version: May 28, 2020

Ryan J-W Smith
C/o British Talent Agency
www.britishtalent.net
0208 123 9110

Sweet Love Adieu

© COPYRIGHT 1999 - 2023, Ryan J-W Smith

Duckpaddle Publishing Ltd.
www.ryanjwsmith.com www.rogueshakespeare.com

Sweet Love Adieu

- NOMINATED -
THE INTERNATIONAL AWARD
HOLLYWOOD FRINGE 2016

"a non-stop, hilarious, irreverent (if not fully raunchy) parody… a loving tribute to the Bard of Avon, from Smith – a bard in his own right… GET YOUR TICKETS NOW!"
LA Stage Reviews

"Smart, funny, bawdy, awesome! There is so much comedic brilliance in the writing and in the performances. My words fail me, Ryan J-W Smith's never do. Go if you possibly can!"
Amy Francis Schott - LA Critic

"Definitely Shakespeare for a modern audience"
UK Theatre Network

"Takes one of Shakespeare's greatest tragedies and turns it into a hilarious comedy…unremitting excellence"
British Theatre Guide

"Farcical, bawdy, a treat! A great piece of entertainment"
Three Weeks

"There IS culture… highly accomplished… this play's a comic delight"
St. Albans Observer

"Methinks it's a treat!"
The Whitby Gazette

"Great fun"
The Stage

The world premiere of Sweet Love Adieu (original version) took place in the Roman Amphitheatre, St. Albans, England in July, 2001.

Lance Frantzich as Magistrate and Ryan J-W Smith as Sidney in the world premiere of Smith's Sweet Love Adieu (version II), McCadden Theatre, Hollywood, CA, 2016.

Ryan J-W Smith backstage as 'William' in his Sweet Love Adieu in 2001.

Dramatis Personae

WILLIAM, a poet
LATIMER, his friend
RIDLEY, his friend / DOCTOR / PRIEST / MAGISTRATE
ANNE, Lord Edmund's ward
AUDREY, cousin to Anne
FAITH, cousin to Anne
LORD EDMUND of Essex
SIDNEY, Lord Edmund's man servant
CHORUS (typically played seamlessly, without costume change, by the actor playing 'Sidney')

Scene: Essex, England.

House lights up.

PROLOGUE

    Enter Chorus.
CHORUS. I pray ye welcome all to this night's play…
    He drops the showmanship - determined to be honest.
God's teeth, I wish ye'd been here yesterday!
Rogue Shakespeare played MacDeth with comic force:
A funny farce? The audience was hoarse!
The critics cheered with fervour rarely seen;
The sexual innuendo is obscene!
There's kilts and cat-suits; cleavages and meat:
One woman in the front row wet her seat!
I could not tell if it was pee – or, not;
10   Is that the greatest compliment or what?!
But now, alas, we must present *this* show;
If you have just walked in, I pray ye, go!
This thing is bawdy; saucy, filthy art!
Don't say I didn't warn you! O, let's start!
                     Exit Chorus.

House lights down.

I.1   *Enter Ridley and Latimer with swords and beer tankards.*
      RIDLEY. Sir Latimer, I prithee, target this.
      LATIMER. Sir Ridley, chum, for thee I shall not miss!
      RIDLEY. How is't our friend, poor William, much of late
      Doth give up sweet delight to seek a mate,
      And for the sake of mating that "he loves"
      Hath bound himself to her, like dullard doves?
      He shuns his friends -
      LATIMER.   And duty to his mind!
      RIDLEY. Now writing endless sonnets of some kind!
      LATIMER. Indeed, I cannot say. 'Tis much he dares;
10   A boy be better by each breast he bares!
      To fall for love is like to beg for pain;
      A gentlemen should *gently* grab her mane,
      And bend her over -
      RIDLEY.   Swift into delight!
      LATIMER. There is no reason, thence, to stay the night!
      RIDLEY. Once business done, give thanks and dress and leave!
      LATIMER. To linger is to her and self deceive!
      RIDLEY. So oft to him this truth imparted I.
      LATIMER. A girlfriend or a wife? I'd rather die!
      RIDLEY. I fear our days of drink and lust are gone!
20   LATIMER. With William, aye, three weeks and yet not one!
      RIDLEY. Wouldst thou believe a man could change so much?
      LATIMER. And all for that which any man could touch!
      RIDLEY. I swear the self-same rumour I have heard.
      LATIMER. An early bloomer, she – that is the word.
      RIDLEY. I had her once or twice, myself, you know.
      LATIMER. I too, she knows a whistle from a blow!
Enter William, above.
      RIDLEY. Alas, great William, now a lovesick fool!
      LATIMER. He comes! I say, let's mock a deadly duel
      And thus invoke his guilt, and shame of heart!
30   RIDLEY. 'Tis well agreed.
      LATIMER. *(Aloud)*   Thou villain!
      RIDLEY. *(Aloud)*   Thou braggart!
      I say our William, friend, will not forget
      The love of us – your insult you'll regret!
      LATIMER. I think not so! He does not care for I;
      He left me here a month that I may die
      In duelling thee, a fool who cannot see:
      Where's William now? He's not with you or me!
          They fight

RIDLEY. I know he hath been vacant much this week:
Some birds will take a cage to dip their beak!
LATIMER. But yesterday he did not show at all:
40   For flakiness your steadfastness shall fall!
         They fight
WILLIAM. *(Aside)* Be there no queens to sweat their heated brow,
That earnestly they fight for my love now?
RIDLEY. *(Aside to Latimer)* The idiot is bated!
LATIMER. *(Aside to Ridley)*   Let's play on!
RIDLEY. *(Aside to Latimer)* I'll parry and riposte.
LATIMER. *(Aside to Ridley)*   I trip – you've won!
         They fight. Latimer falls.
LATIMER. O no! I fell!
RIDLEY.   I have you at my point!
LATIMER. Then spill my blood – his villainy anoint!
         William comes forward.
WILLIAM. Pierce not this anguished heart, Ridley, for me!
For friendship of ye both I here do plea:
I have of late ill-loved ye both, 'tis true,
50   Yet not so much to warrant murder new!
Benet thyself, 'till I requite ye both.
RIDLEY. Ok.
         Ridley helps Latimer to his feet. William approaches.
LATIMER.   Here comes another boundless oath!
WILLIAM. I thank ye, precious friends, I have been blind,
Yet let me mend your aching peace of mind
Conveying unto ye my soul's diffuse:
Into a speech my state I shall reduce.
Two loves have I to guide me in this life:
My Lady, first, perchance to be my wife!
My kinsmen, too, in whom ye both art best,
60   But now these loves against themselves contest.
Mine angel, Hannah, purest of the pure!
LATIMER. I have to interject!
RIDLEY.   Yes, are you sure?
WILLIAM. She promised me her lips have never kissed!
LATIMER. *(Aside)* She took me by the hand.
RIDLEY. *(Aside)*   Can I say, "fist"?
WILLIAM. Her virgin thighs I parted yesternight.
LATIMER. *(Aside)* No man could ever call this woman tight!
WILLIAM. I hope that she may "husband" call me soon.
RIDLEY. *(Aside)* I heard she had a unit – a platoon!
WILLIAM. All others – incomparable, of course.

70   LATIMER. *(Aside)* To satisfy, I fear she needs a horse!
WILLIAM. I worship her, as monks in deepest prayer.
RIDLEY. *(Aside)* I had her on the floor; the bed, the stair!
WILLIAM. My wits this month were dull and could not see,
I'faith, I have of late neglected ye.
The balance of my loves disjointed tell,
But take these words – have wounds attended well:
I will tonight go with ye into town!
Nay, do not look so smug, nor 'gin to frown!
Tonight we'll venture to the ball in masks,

80   See what chance, peradventure, of us asks,
And there my true love Hannah too shall come,
Whose beauty turneth genius to dumb!
RIDLEY. Pray, do forgive my interjection, friend,
Could you repeat that section – near the end?
WILLIAM. From where? "We'll venture to the ball" – that part?
RIDLEY. Aye, there. We have the middle and the start.
WILLIAM. Tonight we'll venture to the ball in masks,
See what chance, peradventure, of us asks,
And there my true love Hannah too shall come,

90   Whose beauty turneth genius to dumb!
RIDLEY. Aye there! That's it! The rub! Do I but dream?
LATIMER. I mentioned his addiction was extreme.
RIDLEY. Indeed, fair Latimer, I owe thee pains!
LATIMER. A shadow of a man, 'tis all remains!
RIDLEY. He comes to us at last and then he says -
LATIMER. With lines from all the best forgotten plays!
RIDLEY. The time has passed, and come, and now I'm back!
LATIMER. "Whose beauty turneth genius?" The hack!
RIDLEY. And look, I'm here among you!
LATIMER   With my Lord!

100   RIDLEY. She has him by the curlies!
LATIMER   By the sword!
WILLIAM. She's not my Lord!
LATIMER.   And yet she comes tonight?
RIDLEY. Tonight is for the boys!
WILLIAM.   All right! All right!
I shall convey a message to my sweet:
      William takes out his cell phone. Sends a text.
"Tonight my hair needs washing."
LATIMER. *(Aside)*   How discreet!
RIDLEY. Where be this ball for maskers that you spoke?
WILLIAM. Lord Edmund's mansion, past the mighty oak,

Where Sally took our cash and spread her legs!
RIDLEY. I had her first!
LATIMER.   I next!
WILLIAM. *(Aside)*   I got the dregs!
RIDLEY. So let us to the theatre.
Exit Ridley.
LATIMER.   Then to ball!
Exit Latimer.
Enter Anne, Faith and Audrey.
110   WILLIAM. Like French, we're all for one and one for all!
Exit William.
ANNE. Upon my throbbing legs! Faith, who was that?
FAITH. Who?
AUDREY.   What?
ANNE.   That man – I'd love to have a chat!
There! There! You see him?
AUDREY.   O aye!
FAITH.   O, I say!
ANNE. Who is he?
AUDREY.   I've not seen afore today.
ANNE. O Lord! Look off! He's coming back.
FAITH.   What, now?
AUDREY. To what, Anne, should we look?
ANNE.   To yonder cow!
FAITH. My legs are sleeping much.
ANNE.   I'll give you hell!
Enter Ridley, Latimer and William crossing the stage.
          Audrey and Anne gaze into the audience. Faith does not.
AUDREY. *(frozen)* I'm not a natural!
FAITH. *(curtsying)*   Monsieur.
WILLIAM. *(bowing)*   Mademoiselle.
Exit Ridley, Latimer and William.
FAITH. O Audrey! Anne! I think I know him well!
120   ANNE. You know him? How?
AUDREY. *(Aside)*   O here we go!
ANNE.   Do tell!
FAITH. His name is William.
AUDREY.   O, how British!
ANNE.   O!
I pray you have not swallowed him?
FAITH. *(insincerely)*   O no!
AUDREY. Be he the one you walked with yesterweek,
Or he the man you shopped with, for antique,

Or be he that which called for you last night?
ANNE. Do not say yes!
AUDREY. *(Aside)*   I think I sense a fight!
FAITH. I met him in the market place, one day;
He's joyful, but I know he is not gay.
By that I mean he's happy and yet sad.
130   AUDREY. Amend your artful speech!
ANNE.   I'm getting mad!
FAITH. He walked me, like a gallant, passed the muck.
AUDREY. I do not like your aim here.
ANNE.   Did you -
FAITH. *(sexually, to annoy Anne)*   "Duck!"
He cried. A mighty arrow hit the tree!
That shaft was almost buried into me!
My body shook, the shock was all too strong;
The size of it – I tell ye, it was long!
My fingers touched, and how my eyes did weep:
To think of it right now – it was so deep!
I thanked him, hard, for saving me my grace,
140   He gave me then a cloth, to wipe my face,
And parted we, as friends, and nothing more.
AUDREY. A happy ending then!
ANNE.   You little whore!
FAITH. How could you think that I, a maiden true,
Could do the slutty things you long to do?
ANNE. The truth is poorly hidden in your speech!
AUDREY. My cousins, please, no fighting – I beseech!
ANNE. Then tell me, Faith, what business does he do?
AUDREY. *(To Anne)* I would not ask for more, if I were you.
FAITH. He is, he claims, a poet of some sort,
150   Though I know nought by whom these works are bought,
Except the untrained ear of those he woos,
Who focus on his waist, and then their shoes!
ANNE. That he's a poet skilled I do not doubt,
But of your arrow-talk, I'll pull that out:
When next I chance I'll ask him to his face,
If then I spy some signal of disgrace
I shall commend thee up and down the land,
But if thou speaketh false I shall thee brand
A coward and a liar! But I'm sure
160   That you have spoken true – a girl so pure!
And yet, I think on all the men I see,
In every case, I swear - or is it me,

You seem to know them deep, and hard and fast:
I think your game is done – this was the last!
(mocking) I do not care if you have stroked his bow,
Or kissed his fletching till his sinew grow,
Or let him put his arrow to your nock,
If you were bound by stringer; gagged by sock!
(attacking) I care not if your well-used quiver felt
170   The weight of every bolt he ever dealt;
Or if your target, large as it may be,
Was ever in his path – it moves not me!
(insincerely) I only care that we remain dear friends!
AUDREY. Enough about all men – now make amends.
FAITH. If I have erred, I pray, forgive me, Anne,
I did not know your feelings for this man.
Enter Edmund, with Sidney who carries a large bag of coals.
EDMUND. Your sentiments for whom?
ANNE.   Lord Edmund, O!
EDMUND. Expound upon this matter – I would know
What man it is 'bout which good Faith just spake?
180   ANNE. There is no other man -
EDMUND.   For pity's sake!
Do not entice my vehemence regrown!
I raised you, girl, as if you were my own:
Your father was a thief, that I had shot,
Yet took I pains to fill your mother's pot,
Ungrateful as she was I forced my load,
Though she would call me murderer and toad,
I sent my servant – burdened down with food,
I strapped her up, though she was ever rude,
And took a trifle token for the rent;
190   It was for you – a charity well spent,
So ye would not go hungry thus and starve!
Perchance one day a craftsman yet may carve
Our wedding bed, I know you would delight
In sitting on my knee most every night,
And playing with my heavy, manly jewels:
It is the only way my temper cools!
And so, my ward, to thee, I here command:
What other man was spoken on – expand!
And do not try to play with words too nice:
200   I am thy master – tell me of thy vice!
AUDREY. My Lord, good Anne, is timid – far too sweet,
Of her amour, she truly did entreat

That we should keep our silence till our graves,
And yet I see this promise all enslaves,
So I shall tell thee whom she doth adore:
FAITH. What are you doing?
ANNE.   Audrey, I implore!
EDMUND. Be quiet, all, and let the lady talk!
AUDREY. She loves his eyes; his elegance, his walk;
She muses on this vision, day and night,
210 And finds herself transfixed upon his sight.
EDMUND. Who is this vile creature – he shall die!
AUDREY. Yourself, my Lord.
EDMUND.   I'll crush his balls!
  Unexpectedly, Edmund strikes Sidney in the crotch.
  Sidney drops the sack of coals.
SIDNEY.   Sir, why?
  Sidney slowly sinks to the floor, holding his crotch.
EDMUND. O wait, her ardour looks upon my gait?
AUDREY. Her ceaseless love towards thee is so great,
She took this time to school us on love's path.
EDMUND. O Anne, my dear, forgive my jealous wrath!
ANNE. 'Tis nothing, sir, a note of passion true,
But now, for modesty, I'll say adieu.
EDMUND. Of course, my love, away now with my praise.
  Anne, Audrey and Faith curtsey.
220 ANNE. May heaven soon reward thy special ways.
    Exit Anne, Audrey and Faith.
EDMUND. O stop! I blush! I blush! But quite, well said!
(Aside) I cannot wait to bend her in my bed!
Well, Sidney, that was splendid, don't you think?
  Sidney is getting up from the floor, with the bag of coals.
SIDNEY. My Lord, I fear I have begun to sink.
EDMUND. What? Wherefore are you sinking, man – speak plain:
Have you been at my whiskey, yet again?
SIDNEY. Thy sack of coals, my Lord, is hard to bear.
EDMUND. Then set it down a moment – over there!
  Sidney instantly drops the bag of coals.
SIDNEY. *(Approaching)* If I may be so bold, can I suggest
230 We keep your winning hand against my chest:
By that I mean I watch young Lady Anne,
Lest she be playing elsewhere?
EDMUND.   Ay, good man!
For virtue, and for honour of my nob!
SIDNEY. For that *(aside)* and coz I hate this bloody job,

(To Edmund) I will observe her at all times of day
To hold your false competitors at bay!
EDMUND. My god! That is a sacred, holy plan,
For there be none as juicy as mine Anne!
SIDNEY. *(Aside)* Quite!
EDMUND .   Right! Come, let us speak within my grange:
240   I have a mighty ball – you must arrange!
                                    Exeunt.
I.2   *Enter Ridley, Latimer and William wearing masks.*
        Latimer's mask has an enormous nose.
        RIDLEY. I have to say, my friend, I like your mask.
        LATIMER. I think that it could serve a double task!
                Ridley pushes up his mask.
        RIDLEY. I doubt it not, though which would have it best?
                William pushes up his mask.
        WILLIAM. I swear to God, on dildos you're obsessed!
                Latimer pushes up his mask.
        LATIMER. This from a man so governed by his crotch;
        Predictable, that I could set my watch:
        Like clockwork, every month, he falls once more,
        Yet every girl he chases is a whore!
        WILLIAM. How dare you call my Hannah by that name!
10   The others? Ay, perhaps – she's not the same!
        LATIMER. What makes you truly certain in this case?
        WILLIAM. She has a sweet and pure angelic face!
        RIDLEY. She works here in the theatre selling fruit:
        If penises were feet she'd be a boot!
        LATIMER. O heaven help this idiot! This lamb!
        If she gave birth by me, you'd push the pram!
        WILLIAM. I will not let ye sully how I see:
        I know she loves and worships only me!
                Ridley has been examining the audience.
        RIDLEY. Is that her there?
        WILLIAM.   What?
        RIDLEY.   There, towards the back.
20   I recognise her figure.
        LATIMER.   That's her rack!
        WILLIAM. What! Where? I cannot see – it is too dark!
        RIDLEY. Pray, house lights going up, then – on my mark!
                The house lights go up.
        She's there, her legs akimbo – see the box?
        LATIMER. *(Aside)* I think we know how Hannah got the pox!
        WILLIAM. *(To Hannah)* Who is that man assailing you; the brute!

RIDLEY. Her mouth is full – effectively she's mute.
WILLIAM. Unhand her, villain! Let me off the stage!
LAT. *(Stopping him)* You cannot leave – the writer pays per page!
WILLIAM. What is he doing now?
RIDLEY.   She's on the floor.
30   LATIMER. Some states consider that against the law!
WILLIAM. I cannot look, my bride to be is cheap!
RIDLEY. We'll commentate.
LATIMER.   He's teasing.
RIDLEY.   No -
LATIMER & RIDLEY.   Balls deep!
      William shrieks
LAT. Let's bring the house lights down!
      The house lights go down. Ridley protests.
                    (to William) Come, come, my friend,
She's but an orange seller – let it end!
Forget this dirty trollop.
WILLIAM. *(To Hannah)* FILTHY SLUT!
RIDLEY. *(Aside)* That's got me in the mood!
WILLIAM. *(in disbelief)*   My baps! My butt!
How could she rent her body in this way?
RIDLEY. Relax, old chum! A fruity girl will stray!
LATIMER. The gentle sex is nothing of the sort.
40   RIDLEY. I think on them, without the aid of thought.
LATIMER. He speaketh sooth, so let us to the ball!
      He pulls his mask back onto his face.
                                    Exit Latimer.
RIDLEY. A man must learn to heed the roaming call!
      He pulls his mask back onto his face.
                                    Exit Ridley.
WILLIAM. I shall go with, but girls I shall not seek.
Why look at Hannah, bouncing! O, the cheek!
      He pulls his mask back onto his face.
                                    Exit William.
I.3   *Enter Lord Edmund and Sidney.*
Both are wearing masks pushed up on their heads.
      EDMUND. O, wherefore must I give these silly balls
      And clutter up my rather splendid halls
      With rabble depravation – middle class:
      It's like an actor sticking in my arse!
      SIDNEY. Thou art the Lord for four and twenty mile,
      And all the rustics love thy special style!
      Politically I also must here state:

Lord Donald hath been generous of late;
The Queen is much in favour of thy foe;
10   These balls are necessary, for they show
How opulent and principal you be:
Think not of self, but of thy family.
EDMUND. But every time it costs me more and more:
I gave you twenty pounds to fill the floor
With heavy tables – look upon that feast,
And yet I sense that I enjoy the least!
SIDNEY. Thy virtue is a lesson to us all:
There is no height from which our love could fall;
We gaze from low upon a man so high -
20   Are you an angel, sir? Come, don't deny!
EDMUND. I must admit, I do believe it so:
I am the most delightful man I know!
Thou didst invite my youngest prize, fair Anne?
I chance to have her please me, if I can:
I'll lure her to my chamber for a drink;
For billiards, perchance to sink the pink!
The thought of that young body on my mast!
O no, I think I'm – O God! That was fast!
SIDNEY. Rest well, my eager Lord, I spy her there.
30   EDMUND. I need to find a bathroom!
Exit Edmund.
SIDNEY. *(Aside)*   I despair!
Exit Sidney.
Enter Ridley, Latimer and William with masks pushed up.
WILLIAM. I cannot yet believe my Hannah would -
She does not act the way a sweet girl should!
Perhaps she merely fell into his lap,
And did not wish for him her arse to slap,
And plunder fondly, as he clearly did?
LATIMER. Her treachery was not a thing well-hid!
WILLIAM. Perchance she loves me truly, but she's scared;
Deliberately she sabotaged! She cared!
RIDLEY. Whatever be the reason, you are free;
40   Take stock of all these beauties – come and see!
They examine the audience.
LATIMER. I like that honey. Second row.
RIDELY.   She's mine!
LATIMER. I'll wager thee a breakfast, I shall dine!
RIDELY. I'll fight thee for her, skivvy!
LATIMER.   Wait, I pass.

RIDELY. What have you now?
LATIMER.   Celebrity.
RIDELY and LATIMER.   That's class!
WILLIAM. O no, I had that journey – venture not:
No handle on reality – the lot!
LATIMER. He could be right. You cannot say them, "nay!"
RIDELY. The rich are very scornful when you stray.
WILLIAM. Come, let us find the bar – I need a beer!

Exit William.

50   LATIMER. I love a buxom waitress!

Exit Latimer.

RIDELY.   Follow near!

Exit Ridley.

Enter Audrey, Anne and Faith with masks pushed up.
ANNE. I know you were just covering, and yet,
I hope your tongue won't cause my lips regret!
AUDREY. I did the best I could, what can I say?
I cannot just invent the perfect play!
FAITH. Lord Edmund will expect thy love to grow;
I'faith, I think he'll want a decent show!
If I were thee I'd buy a lock and key
And bolt secure thy sacred chastity.
I'd also keep that mask upon thy face.
60   AUDREY. I have a taser!
FAITH.   Look, I carry mace!
ANNE. I hope and pray it will not come to that.
FAITH. I know a guy who's handy with a bat!
AUDREY. I'll bet you do!
ANNE.   He's just a lonely man.
AUDREY. I would not be so generous!
FAITH.   O Anne!
ANNE. Let's try, at least, to still enjoy this night.
FAITH. Then we must keep you guarded.
AUDREY.   Faith is right!
We must not let him separate our herd.
FAITH. Or separate your legs!
ANNE.   That is preferred!
Enter Sidney, wearing his mask.
          Faith, Audrey and Anne put on their masks.
AUDREY. Come, let us find some revellers to dance.

Exit Audrey.

70   FAITH. Perchance a gallant Knight!

Exit Faith.

ANNE.   No more romance!
          Exeunt all but Sidney.
   Sidney pushes up his mask.
SIDNEY. Ah yes, I see the target for my Lord:
One thing about this job – I'm never bored!
I know just what you're thinking, but you're wrong:
You think that I am weakly – I am strong!
You see a servant, at his master's tip?
Before he takes his drink, I take my sip.
In sooth, I am a businessman, of sort,
This act of lower class is all for sport;
I have more money than I care to say,

80 But why give up the wealth of where I stay?
I like it here, the décor is quite grand:
My quarters better yours – you understand?
I take a little here, I save and scheme;
Relationships are never what they seem.
So take a look at them beside you now:
The bull may go before the tilling plough,
But who is working harder; who's relaxed?
When things are given free they are not taxed!
The rich are often stupid with their wealth:

90 The poor can change their lot though cunning stealth.
So play the part of pauper – it's a game!
Allow the rich their rank, there is no shame
In conning these felonious tight gits!
What they have in their banks we have in wits.
Hush! Quiet now, let's keep our secret safe:
Upon the skin of opulence, we chafe!
Enter Lord Edmund, holding his mask.
EDMUND. O Sidney, there you are my special chap!
I lay down on my bed – I took a nap!
I could not clean my trousers like you can;

100 You know I need my trusty servant man!
SIDNEY. Relax, my grace, your stature hides your mess;
Your child bride, she doth wander in distress;
The monarchy is pleased you threw the ball:
Now let's advance the plot – nay, do not stall!
I shall distract her kinfolk - Audrey, Faith,
So you might take advantage of the waif,
And if you were to give me five pound more,
I'll keep them busy, till you make her sore!
   Edmund gives Sidney money.

EDMUND. I like a bargain, Mister!
SIDNEY. *(Aside)*   So do I!
110   EDMUND. Do keep her kinfolk occupied!
SIDNEY.   I'll try!
They're coming back, my Lord, put on your mask,
(Aside) Whilst I perform this small, but well-paid, task.
                    Sidney and Edmund put on their masks.
Enter Faith, Anne and Audrey wearing their masks.
O welcome, ladies. Tell me, how's the night?
FAITH. The champagne is delightful!
ANNE.   True!
AUDREY.   Quite right!
Sidney puts an arm around Audrey, and another around Faith.
SIDNEY. And did ye note the audience we gained?
Despite the innuendo some remained!
FAITH. O look! I see some gentlemen of class.
AUDREY. It's good to know the upper crust like farce!
SIDNEY. And did ye see the banquet hall just yet?
120   I hear the dinner table has been set.
FAITH. I'd love a meaty sausage!
AUDREY.   I want pie!
SIDNEY. Whate'er your heart could wish for, we supply!
                    Exit Sidney, Audrey and Faith.
            Edmund approaches Anne using a different accent.
EDMUND. Where are you going, Lady?
ANNE.   With my friends.
EDMUND. I hoped you might escort me?
ANNE.   To what ends?
EDMUND. I would invite thee – leave these sycophants:
To join another party - in my pants!
ANNE. I'm sorry! Come again?
EDMUND. *(aside)*   I hope to soon!
ANNE. I'm not that type of girl.
EDMUND.   Then we can spoon!
ANNE. I really must be going.
EDMUND. *(pushing up his mask)* Not so fast!
130   ANNE. O my! Lord Edmund!
EDMUND.   Ah, alone at last!
Come with me now, dear girl.
ANNE.   Ahhh!
EDMUND.   Do not cry:
I have a thing for you, you'll not deny!
                    Exit Edmund leading Anne.

Enter Faith, Audrey and Sidney.
Faith and Audrey have pushed up their masks.

       FAITH. I do not doubt your morals, gentle man,
       But we are three! O Audrey, where is Anne?
       AUDREY. O Faith, I do not see her anywhere!
       We charged ourselves to keep her in our care!
       SIDNEY. I doubt she could be far – let's look within.
       AUDREY. The audience?
       FAITH.   I'm seeing vice and sin!
       SIDNEY. How many in tonight?
       AUDREY.   I cannot sum.
140   SIDNEY. Is that a noble countess?
       FAITH.   That's my mum!
       AUDREY. O Faith, how did we come to this defeat?
       FAITH. This person did invite us come and eat.
       SIDNEY. Now ladies, do not look that way at me,
       As if I could be part of villainy!
       AUDREY. The mask you're wearing – take it off your head!
       FAITH. I kept a knife from dinner!
       AUDREY.   As I said,
       Remove your mad disguise so we can know!
            Sidney pushes up his mask.
       FAITH. It's Sidney!
       AUDREY.   He's Lord Edmund's lackey!
       FAITH and AUDREY.   NOOO!
Enter Ridley, Latimer and William wearing masks.
       LATIMER. Sweet Ladies, what's the matter?
       RIDLEY.   What has passed?
150   FAITH. A sausage tempted me!
       AUDREY.   She's perfect cast!
       FAITH. We have been tricked and lost our cousin's fate.
       AUDREY. Pray help us, sirs, before it is too late.
       FAITH. He means to have her, like a thieving cad!
       AUDREY. O hurry, sirs, 'afore we must say "had!"
       FAITH. Please help us find our friend, sweet Lady Anne.
       AUDREY. Lord Edmund is the rogue!
       WILLIAM.   I have a plan!
       Let's all split up and seek Lord Edmund out,
       So of his scheme to bed her, we can rout!
       LATIMER. It might just work!
       RIDLEY.   It's genius!
       LATIMER.   What wits!
160   WILLIAM. We must not let him stroke or squeeze her -

RIDLEY.   Bits!
LATIMER. Agreed!
RIDLEY.   I shall go this way.
AUDREY.   Yes, I too.
Exit Ridley and Audrey.
FAITH. *(To Latimer)* I'll follow thee.
LATIMER.   My Lady.
FAITH.   After you!
Exit Latimer and Faith.
WILLIAM. What know thee of this, scoundrel?
SIDNEY.   She's down there.
WILLIAM. Much thanks! I now shall rescue!
Exit William.
SIDNEY.   Mind the stair!
Loud noises off - a crash and fall.
WILLIAM. *(Off)* I am ok! I'm good! I struggle on!
SIDNEY. The stage is bare of wits when I am gone.
Exit Sidney.

I.4 *Enter Lord Edmund leading Anne. Both have lost their masks.*
EDMUND. Now here regard my bounteous great halls;
No other person sees these in my balls!
All marble gilded and pure gold throughout,
Which hold, moreover, precious stones on mount.
Each ruby, diamond, sapphire and rare gem,
Denotes the class and wealth from which I stem.
'Tis quite a thing to be a noble Lord,
To know thy humble self is so adored!
Thy love for me I treasure more than wealth;
10 I mean to have thee willing, *(aside)* or by stealth!
(to Anne) But either way, I grow to have thee now:
Give up your milky bits you dirty cow!
Nay, do not struggle so – it does not help;
Until my man is entered, do not yelp!
My sweet amour; my little girl, be calm!
Resist me not! Stop biting! That's my arm!
I see you like it rough? I shan't deny:
If you demand a master, I'll supply!
Edmund forces Anne down until she is hidden behind some piece of furniture
or part of the set, and cannot be seen by the audience.
I have you now! So sink into your place:
20 Now open wide and take it – use your face!
O yes! O yes! Keep going! Wait! O No!
That's hurting! No! You're biting! Let me go!

Edmund moves downstage, his hands on his crotch.
>My manhood! O my little chap is hurt!
Anne rises up, her lips bloodied.
>What's wrong with you? Sweet romance you pervert!
>I need to find a doctor in the house,
>And double-think upon my future spouse!
>>*Exit Lord Edmund*

Enter William, wearing his mask.
>WILLIAM. Are you the gentle maiden they call Anne?
>>*Anne spits out blood.*
>ANNE. *(Aside)* O good, just what I need – another man!
>WILLIAM. If you be she I came to rescue straight!
>>*Anne wipes her bloody face.*

30   ANNE. Your timing could be better – you are late!
>WILLIAM. You mean, he had his false and wicked way?
>>*Anne finds something between her teeth.*
>ANNE. Not quite. In fact I think he'll rue the day.
>WILLIAM. You have your humour, thus, you have your pride?
>ANNE. In plainest speech – he did not get inside!
>WILLIAM. O thank the Lord for mercies, here beneath!
>ANNE. The Lord did nought – I had to use my teeth!
>But who art thou? Remove thy mask and show.
>WILLIAM. I hope to be a gentleman you know.
>>*William removes his mask.*
>ANNE. I recognise – it's William, correct?
>>*William strikes a super-hero pose.*

40   WILLIAM. A poet, with a duty to protect!
>ANNE. Pray, do you know my cousin, her name's Faith?
>She is so high; her birthday is the eighth?
>She has a mole right here upon her breast.
>>*William reacts.*
>I see you know her – what an easy test!
>And sure, you practise archery, no doubt:
>Her bullseye – are you in or are you out?
>>*William remembers, with enthusiasm.*
>WILLIAM. I may have known your cousin, long ago,
>As I recall, I met her in the snow;
>She took me – to a stable, I was brung:

50   She's talented, and gracious with her tongue!
>ANNE. Enough! I do not need to hear this yarn;
>I know the girl, the legend and the barn!
>WILLIAM. I pray it will not taint your view of me?
>ANNE. I have no view, Monsieur, now let me be.

WILLIAM. So be it, Mademoiselle, I'll say adieu;
I wish you well in everything you do.
ANNE. Yes, do not try to woo me, sir. Goodbye!
WILLIAM. I do not seek where seeking would deny.
ANNE. O leave me, sir!
WILLIAM.   I'm going!
ANNE.   Do not stay!
60   WILLIAM. Do you not see me walking?
ANNE.   Wait, I pray!
        William trips, then recovers.
Perchance you could consider, as you stall,
That I, in sooth, would ask that you might call
Unto my door – a date tomorrow eve;
Assuming you're not busy, to receive?
WILLIAM. I am a little hazy – you want me
To call for you tomorrow; us to be
A couple on a night of drink and fun?
ANNE. I know I have been frosty – do not shun.
Lord Edmund; Faith; experience can taint
70   But you are fair, *(aside)* and I have been no saint!
So let us try this different – I shall woo,
If you, kind sir, would hence permit me to?
        William is confused
WILLIAM. How can I say thee "no" – you are too sweet!
ANNE. Then come and kiss me, love – from head to feet!
        Anne grabs William. They kiss, with ridiculously
        inappropriate familiarity.
One other thing – quite soon we should be wed!
Lord Edmund, based on all that hath been said,
Is set upon my person as his bride:
I cannot run away; we cannot hide!
'Tis only through another husband I
80   Could face his suit, and legally deny.
WILLIAM. Then I shall wake a priest that I well know!
ANNE. I do beseech thee, kiss me love!
        Anne grabs and kisses William again.
ANNE.   Now go!
        Anne pushes William away.
WILLIAM. Until tomorrow, angel of the ball!
                              Exit William.
ANNE. My husband is most handsome, and quite tall!
Enter Faith and Latimer, unmasked.
FAITH. O Anne, you're safe and sound! I pray, what passed?

Is everything intact?
ANNE.   I'm glad you asked:
I met your snowy conquest, from the barn.
FAITH. So many of your socks I hence shall darn
If you would keep your silence, we've a guest!
90   This is sweet, Latimer.
ANNE.   You do not rest!

Enter Audrey and Ridley, unmasked.

AUDREY. O Anne, my dear! Thank God you are with friends!
ANNE. Upon a definition that depends,
But yes, I'm well, and we should leave in haste:
Lord Edmund is not well below the waist!
His wrath will fall upon me, lest we part.
LATIMER. We shall attend.
RIDELY.   Let's rob a horse and cart!
LATIMER. Good thinking, Ridley!
RIDLEY.   We shall lead the way!
                                    Exeunt all but Faith.
FAITH. *(Aside)* The plot is getting thicker – won't you stay?
                                        Exit Faith.

Enter Chorus. He cleans the blood on the floor with a mop.
> CHORUS. Our star-crossed lovers at a ball have met,
> On paradise, their aching hearts are set,
> They stole new fortune with a sacred kiss -
> I tell ye, so original is this!
> Have ye not heard of Romeo, my dear,
> And Juliet, by someone called Shakespeare?
> I grant ye, all the lines are mighty fresh,
> > *Picking a lady in the front row.*
> And I can tell, she's liking all the flesh!
> I told you it was dirty, didn't I?
> She's running like a faucet – don't deny!
> Ah yes, the plot, I shall to ye impart:
> Since William has left his latest tart
> He seeks to marry Anne, or she does him,
> But that depends on Edmund and his whim.
> > > *Exit Chorus.*

10

II.1   *Enter Doctor and Sidney.*
        SIDNEY. How is his poorly pecker, doctor, state?
        DOCTOR. He lost a lot of blood; we'll have to wait.
        SIDNEY. He caught it in his zipper – not Anne's face!
        DOCTOR. I saw a lot of teeth marks near the base!
        SIDNEY. O no, you are mistaken doctor, sure;
        Nobility is innocent and pure!
        For there to be a bite about his lance
        There'd have to be a biter – there's no chance,
        For he is long enamoured of his wife,
10   And though she lives abroad, upon my life,
        He would not dare to lose her fortune, see!
        The things you saw let's keep 'twixt you and me.
        Here, take a sovereign for thy troubled mind;
                Sidney tempts the doctor with a coin.
        His Lordship to his friends can be most kind:
        That placement in the hospital you seek,
        We'll see to your promotion, come next week.
        Imagine all the crumpet you'll command:
        The nurses' god! – I knew you'd understand.
                Sidney gives the doctor the coin.
        Now leave us, so his Lordship can get well;
20   Remember, there is nothing here to tell!
                     Exit Doctor.
        I thus protect my dinner and my plate,
        And watch me make more money, for I'll state,
        "Lord Edmund, grace, I gave him several pound;
        The doctor is on-side – I brought him round!"
        Well, wherefore should I not increase my stash?
        The currency of silence comes in cash.
Enter Edmund.
        EDMUND. O Sidney, did you calm the doctor down?
        I cannot have him telling all the town!
Sidney speaks looking at the audience with a smile.
        SIDNEY. Lord Edmund, grace, I gave him several pound;
30   The doctor is on-side – I brought him round!
        EDMUND. O thank you, Sidney, here's a bag of gold.
Edmund gives Sidney a bag of gold.
        I trust that you will use it thus to mould
        The stories of my injury and pain,
        Into an act of valour, not of shame?
        SIDNEY. Of course, my Lord, your status is my wealth!
        Now please go back to bed: regain your health.

EDMUND. You'll find me Anne, and drag her to my door?
SIDNEY. You are the ruling class – you own the poor!
EDMUND. Go seek the magistrate, and show him this.
    Edmund hands Sidney a letter.
40   If Anne will not give freely, buy my bliss!
                         Exit Edmund.
SIDNEY. An ignorant, conceited, awful punt!
A mucking fuddle! Such a cupid stunt!
                       Exit Sidney.

II.2   *Enter Priest. He sings his own choral entrance music.*
PRIEST. Now I am God's own servant, humble priest,
Unto the loaf of heaven, I'm the yeast!
I am at total peace as here I sit.

Enter William.

WILLIAM. Good morrow, Father!
PRIEST. *(surprised)*   TITS AND HOLY SHIT!
I pray do not excite me thus my son!
You're never here this early – what's begun?
WILLIAM. I met a special lady yesternight;
She wooed me; I am taken!
PRIEST.   Is that right?
WILLIAM. And yet she has a legal case; a plea:
10   She's ward to that Lord Edmund.
PRIEST.   O, I see.
WILLIAM. And so we wish to marry with much haste!
This lady is so perfect: sweet and chaste,
And we must cease his Lordship in his plan
To make a concubine of my love, Anne!
PRIEST. 'Tis quite a situation, I must say,
A plot for what could be the greatest play!
And yet, I have a question, for you boy,
It doth concern our friendship, and your ploy:
I fear that should you take a loyal bride,
20   You may no longer in myself confide;
I'd miss our treasured moments, down below:
Our special education, well, you know.
I want you to be happy, yes, of course,
But what about your holy hobbyhorse?
WILLIAM. O Father, truly, how could I forget,
The grooming of your William – your pet!
It's like I'm in a needy, anxious state
When you remind: my cheeks are your estate!
PRIEST. I sense that all will stay just as it be:

30   As such you have my blessing – come to me
And bring your precious woman to my church,
And we shall end your endless marriage search.
WILLIAM. O thank you, Father! See now how I sweat!
PRIEST. Perhaps because you love her, you're upset?
WILLIAM. That must be it! I'm panicking within!
PRIEST. The church is here to save you from your sin!
WILLIAM. I shall then take my leave until tonight:
Farewell my holy hobbyhorse!
                        Exit William.
PRIEST. *(Aside)*   Quite right!
     Priest sings choral music.   *Exit Priest, singing.*

II.3   *Enter Sidney with a letter.*
SIDNEY. I came me here to find the magistrate,
The time agreed, but clearly he is late;
What could it be that keeps him, I know not?
I hope he does not slow our racing plot!
Perchance he had to change his costume – clothes,
So he would not be noticed, I suppose?
Yet if that be the case, I'll state this clear:
I do not know how long I can stand here
And improvise in perfect, metered verse!
10   *(Aside)* This isn't quite the scene we did rehearse.
(To the wings) No, do not rush yourself, mate, take your time:
I'm handy with my fists as I am rhyme!
Enter Magistrate wearing the Priest's cross.
Ah-ha, he comes! The magistrate, at last!
MAGISTRATE. These changes weren't declared when I was cast!
     Sidney removes the cross and hands it to the Magistrate.
But here I am, the priest – no, magistrate,
Apologising that you had to wait,
(Slowly, uncertain) I had to do some magistrating stuff:
My magistrating days can be quite tough!
SIDNEY. No matter, Justice, take a look at this:
     Sidney gives him the letter.
20   Lord Edmund would the fair maid, Annie, kiss!
MAGISTRATE. But he is married.
SIDNEY.   Could he then adopt?
MAGISTRATE. Well, incest is a crime that can't be stopped!
SIDNEY. Let's keep that in the family, good sir.
MAGISTRATE. I shall prepare the papers to confer
Her personage and all her goods to him.
SIDNEY. I think he's most fixated on her quim!

MAGISTRATE. Whatever part he likes, he'll own it all!
SIDNEY. Perhaps this afternoon you could then call
Unto his Lordships great estate – come quick:

30   So he can mend his status, and his -
MAGISTRATE.   Dick,
My rock-hard young assistant will come too.
This afternoon is fine, round one or two?
SIDNEY. As soon as you can muster sir, I pray.
MAGISTRATE. Until such time, good sir, farewell.
SIDNEY.   Good day!

Exit Magistrate

Let's take a little moment – you and I,
To contemplate the beauty of the sky!
What? No! I'm no theatrical device
To cover Ridley's quick change – that's not nice!
My motivation here is deeply spun:

40   *(into the wings)* You're ready?
RIDLEY. *(off)*   NOT QUITE!
SIDNEY. *(to the audience)*   Why, regard the sun!
Where-ever it may be right now – it shines,
So brightly! Like these high, poetic lines!
If you are ready now just give a cough!

Ridley coughs, off.

The sun has set. I'm leaving - now!

Exit Sidney.

(off) I'M OFF!

II.4   *Enter Ridley and Latimer.*
Ridley is still getting changed as he comes on.

LATIMER. Last night was quite the bold adventure sought;
I still cannot believe we were not caught!
RIDLEY. Where did you hide the carriage that we stole?
LATIMER. I took it back this morning, with the foal,
And all the other horses, where his grace
Rewarded me, and thanked me to my face!
RIDELY. How much then did he give you?
LATIMER.   Half a crown.
What happened to your girl?
RIDLEY.   She tore her gown.
LATIMER. I'll bet she did.
RIDLEY.   It wasn't quite like that.

10   And of the girl you met?
LATIMER.   We had a chat.
RIDLEY. I know your natter always ends up crude!

LATIMER. This one's a little different, don't be rude!
Besides, you're one to talk, when don't you bed
The strumpet that can turn your simple head?
RIDLEY. My Audrey is no strumpet next to yours!
LATIMER. My Faith is pure – shall we take this outdoors?
RIDLEY. Why go outside, I'll end you quickly here!
LATIMER. I love a friend turned enemy – come near!
    They fight.
Enter William, above.
RIDLEY. I'll have you sunshine!
LATIMER.   Have this in thine eye!
20   RIDELY. I'll shove it up your girlfriend!
LATIMER.   You will die!
WILLIAM. *(Aside)* This surely cannot be a real fight.
RIDLEY. O William! Come! I need your help!
WILLIAM. *(calmly)*   All right!
LATIMER. Ay, come and help me kick this villain's butt!
RIDLEY. Your lover is an orange and a slut!
O William, no, he has me in a vice!
I do not wish to die!
WILLIAM.   Ok, that's nice!
LATIMER. I'll choke the very life out of your bones!
Enter Audrey and Faith.
FAITH. What's happening, I pray?
AUDREY.   Such awful groans!
Ridley and Latimer stop fighting.
RIDLEY. Ah, ladies!
LATIMER.   We were training.
RIDLEY.   Nothing more.
30   FAITH. We heard some words like "Jezebel" and "whore"?
LATIMER. A parody of plays from long ago!
WILLIAM. They long to act! I'm William – hello!
    William greets Audrey.
AUDREY. And Audrey, I. Sweet Faith you know, I think?
WILLIAM. 'Twas brief, but yes.
RIDLEY. *(Aside)*   How now?
LATIMER. *(Aside)*   Why does she wink?
FAITH. Alas, we carry ill, disturbing news,
That doth mine eye so fervidly abuse!
Our cousin, Anne, your bride to be is caught!
Lord Edmund, through the magistrate, hath bought
This orphan to be daughter to his grace!
40   To worship him and sit upon his -

AUDREY.   Face
The fearful facts, sweet gentlemen, and act;
We must be quick to circumvent this pact!
WILLIAM. O precious love! I'll gladly give my life
To save my super-duper, future wife!
                                        Exit William.
RIDLEY. Nay, let him solus dwell, my gracious friend.
LATIMER. We must allow this act to somehow end!
RIDLEY. Let's exit here!
AUDREY.   To form a cunning plan!
LATIMER. We'll save the hearts -
FAITH.   Of William, and Anne!
                                        Exeunt all.
House lights up.

INTERVAL

Enter Chorus.

      CHORUS. Come on! Come on, now. Settle down! Be sweet;
      The time has come to get back in your seat!
      You brought a glass of vino? That is smart!
      'Tis best that we imbibe when viewing art,
      And this is barely artistry, I'd say!
      No, do not get me wrong, I like the play,
      And yet I cannot tell if it was writ,
      Or if these rogues just improvise with wit?
      Did anyone here buy the script? The book?
10   You have it there? Pray, can I take a look?
      Now let me find my place – O, here we go:
      "Give back the book and get on with the show!"
      Well, strike a light, this author knows a thing:
      Here, take it back – the puppet saw the string!
                         Exit Chorus.

House lights down.

III.1   *Enter Anne.*
       ANNE. Unhappy me! Already afternoon;
       I pray a hopeful message finds me soon.
       But wherefore art mine cousins yet so late?
       I cannot fadge – they know my woeful state:
       How Edmund hath restricted me to home;
She takes out her cell phone.
       The New World Order tracking should I roam;
       My twitter feed's been censored – FBI,
She tosses her cell phone away.
       And, unexpectedly - I may soon die!
Slight pause. She looks offstage. Then, sincerely:
       We go along to get along, but now
10   I have to speak the truth, my holy vow:
       A plague is here upon us, all man-made;
       I took the so-called cure - I was betrayed!
       When danger from the drug exceeds disease
       'Tis best to trust to nature; not to please
       The profit margins of foul company!
       I wish it were not so, but so it be.
       My friends are falling, left and right, so young;
       I must give voice; I cannot hold my tongue!
       Conspiracists proved right with each new day;
20   There's tragedy in every comic play.
Slight pause. She looks offstage. Then, dramatically:
       O William, wherefore must you be so?
       O come and rescue; Edmund overthrow;
       Climb up and save your princess from her plight -
Anne breaks 'character' and talks to the audience.
       I'm sorry, but these lines are just so trite!
       Do any women talk like this these days?
       It's clear – the writer read some ancient plays,
       But girls are tough and hardy now – I am:
       I've messed this up, but I don't give a damn!
       You want a true performance, set me free:
30   I'll improvise iambic – you shall see!
       Director, writer, sirs, I have a list:
       Bring Edmund to my door, then to my fist!
Enter Lord Edmund. He plays as if Anne has been going off-script.
       EDMUND. Ah, here's our leading, yet inventive girl!
       I come to furnish thee with pretty pearl:
       A necklace for thy neck of lily white;
       And pray that you might get your next speech right!

The one where you relinquish to my weight;
Accepting your replaceable, low state!
Where you will beg and plead upon your knees,
40   And must accept direction, as we please!
ANNE. My instincts tell me I must hold my own;
The nature of this scene I have been shown:
So I will not go gentle through this night -
You want control of me? You've got a fight!
Enter Sidney, unseen above. Anne prepares to fight.
EDMUND. Now, calm yourself, my darling – let's just talk,
It sometimes helps to breathe and take a walk!
ANNE. I'll walk my feet across your lordship's face!
You're shaking at the knees!
Sidney covertly throws a weapon down for Anne.   Exit Sidney, above.
EDMUND. *(leaving)*   You need your space.
'Tis obvious, I'll let you settle down!
      Anne finds and picks up the weapon.
50   ANNE. I'll beat you till your body's black and brown!
      Anne beats Edmund with the weapon.
EDMUND. Get off of me, you crazy little minx!
ANNE. O turn your mouth away from me, it stinks!
EDMUND. I do not wish to hurt you! Let me go!
ANNE. You wanted me to beat you off – ergo!
EDMUND. To scenes rehearsed I would prefer we stick;
It's just so unprofessional!
ANNE.   You prick!
My misandry for thee shall never rest!
Enter Sidney.
EDMUND. O that's my back; my leg; my groin, my chest!
SIDNEY. My Lord! My future income! My device!
60   Hurt not my wealthy master, Anne, be nice!
      Sidney stands between Anne and Edmund.
EDMUND. O Sidney, thank the heavens! She's gone mad!
ANNE. You said you liked a naughty girl – *(aside)* I'm bad!
EDMUND. I do assure thee, Sidney – O my leg!
I say she didst invite me here, nay beg!
She threw me to the wall; I took a knock,
And then she slapped my aching, throbbing -
SIDNEY.   Cock
Your head a little this way, sir, it bleeds.
I full believe she started these misdeeds!
70   ANNE. O!
EDMUND. See thee, how she clamours for my knave!

ANNE. Thou piglet! I'll dispatch thee to thy grave!
EDMUND. She's desperate for my chappie – longs to touch;
I love a wanton tart, but she's too much!
SIDNEY. Your grace, I beg thee, leave me with the girl;
Her fist of iron soon I shall unfurl.
EDMUND. O, thank you, Sidney. Watch your crotch! Take care!
There is no telling what that whore may dare!
                 Exit Edmund.
SIDNEY. Now listen to me, lady. Cool your feet;
80   You need to learn the worth of being sweet!
Be savvy in your enmity - be smart,
Beguiling the nobility's an art!
You think that I enjoy my station here?
I've learned to keep my enemy most near.
So let me help you in this complex plot:
You do not understand the wealth you've got!
As daughter to his Lordship, next in line,
If anything should happen - his decline,
Then you would turn out rich and royalty!
90   You're closer than you think; have faith in me:
I have his trust and I have pains for you;
I tell you, there is nothing he can do!
He's trapped himself; it's over, check-mate – done!
There's just a little intrigue to be spun.
So play your part, be gallant as you wait;
He's always had it coming – this is fate!
Your father was a gentleman, a friend;
His Lordship is about to meet his end.
      Sidney picks up the weapon and moves to the exit.
      (loudly) So, let that be a lesson to you, Anne,
100   Lord Edmund is a prize! A perfect man!
      Sidney winks at Anne.   Exit Sidney, with the weapon.
ANNE. O father! Has it been so long since I
Did fall upon my knees for thee and cry?
And mother, now I understand your flight;
For family your daughter strong will fight!
My ignomy was all by Edmund's hand;
His downfall, by my oath, will be as grand!
So rest ye both, for all shall be set right:
A noble resolution, here – tonight!
                 Exit Anne.
III.2   *Enter William.*
WILLIAM. I had a speech to God upon my lips,

But all of that at present? Merely quips!
Religion is a man-made iron cage
To mute domestic enemies who rage
And use their voice to criticise our lords,
That enter wars and other false accords!
It's always common folk who end up poor:
Austerity when bankers break the law;
Impoverished, we join the army ranks,
10   That fuel the oil wars; fund the off-shore banks,
And it is us – the average man who dies,
Or kills a family from airborne spies,
Because our kings seek plunder from their land:
A hegemonic psychopath – how grand!
Why do we bother? Tell me, what's the point?
Our rulers aren't elect, they self-appoint!
The theatre of establishment is clear:
Two parties in a play – they act sincere,
But I have known the stage for decades now:
20   All actors stand together for the bow!
It's all a fix, you have no say – no vote:
The simple truth is all we simply wrote.
Not one of us will leave here free from sin
Until we see the enemy within.
I speak of revolution? Surely not!
It's just a silly play – a random plot!
Have peace, my copesmates enter in some state;
I'll hide behind the arras, and await.
                    William hides.
Enter Ridley, Latimer, followed by Faith and Audrey.
          LATIMER. But as a woman?
          RIDLEY.   Truly it must be:
30   That we have stolen her they must not see!
One girl they are to coop and one they'll count,
If thou wilt stoop and hide thy monster mount!
I would myself, but that I have a beard,
And as an actor thou art most revered!
          LATIMER. But surely -
          RIDLEY.   Grand! He'll do it! What a man!
          FAITH. O thank you, pretty gentleman, from Anne!
                    Faith kisses Latimer.
          AUDREY. Let's move apace! We must contrive our text,
So that our audience are left perplexed:
Astounded at our genius in verse,

40   In short, let's find a place we can rehearse!
Exit Latimer, Faith and Audrey.
RIDLEY. I'll have to leave them to it – I've this thing:
Another place to be – a dog; a ring;
An acting job, of sorts, I shouldn't state:
Perchance I'll see you soon! *(to the wings)* Ok! *(aside)* I'm late!
Exit Ridley.
William comes forth.
WILLIAM. Respect is something hard to earn these days,
You have to choose your moment, writing plays!
And yet, despite my situation grave:
Nefarious enslavement by a knave,
Just let me think upon what I have heard,
50   Wherefore do friends make merry – 'tis absurd?!
Supplanting duty to their ancient friend,
Metastasising poems!? To what end!?
It cannot be appropriate or right
To think upon the theatre here tonight!
He looks around the theatre.
How can I find the path to fools deny?
The author of this manuscript is I.
Exit William.

III.3   *Enter Lord Edmund, Sidney and Magistrate with a paper and pen.*
SIDNEY. We thank, thee, magistrate for coming swift,
To mend this trivial domestic rift;
His Lordship is most grateful – sign here quick!
Lord Edmund signs the paper – Sidney keeps it.
EDMUND. My signature? Lord Edmund. O my -
SIDNEY.   Dick,
Your hardy young assistant could not come?
MAGISTRATE. He took a nasty fall and hurt his thumb.
SIDNEY. Such injuries, it seems, are spreading fast!
(Aside) Another show like this and I'll recast!
EDMUND. I must return to bed and take a nap!
10   SIDNEY. Rest well, assured, my Lord. We've set the trap!
Exit Edmund.
O magistrate, chief justice, can I ask,
Before we thus conclude our legal task,
Let's add a line: how Anne is his sole heir.
MAGISTRATE. That's normal! Where to add it?
SIDNEY.   O, right there.
MAGISTRATE. I thus amend; initial, all is set.
SIDNEY. That was an act, I'm sure, you won't regret.

MAGISTRATE. Well, I must leave – I moonlight as a priest!
SIDNEY. You service both the living and deceased?
MAGISTRATE. If that's a sexual question, I deny –
20   SIDNEY. No need for you to answer, sir. Goodbye!
                                        Exit Magistrate.
So now we have him, truly in his grave;
But one day more as Edmund's trusty slave!
                                Exit Sidney with the paper.
Enter William.
WILLIAM. Now press forth I, unto my love's estate,
To rescue precious love and to rebate
And blunt Lord Edmund's ill-composèd scheme:
To visit roughly up her gentle seam!
*Enter Anne, above. If there is no balcony available: Anne enters holding a
small block which she, embarrassed, puts on the floor and steps on as if on a
raised balcony.*
        (uncertainly) What! Ho! She's at her balcony above!
*William, looking at the audience, slowly kneels to counter Anne's lack of
balcony height.*
30   My angel! Anne! It's William – your dove!
ANNE. O William!
WILLIAM.   My lover!
ANNE.   Not today!
I have a plan, you blockhead! Go away!
WILLIAM. But I have come to rescue you, my sweet!
ANNE. I do not need your rescue! Pray, retreat!
WILLIAM. But as a man of honour –
ANNE.   Please don't start!
WILLIAM. It is my duty -
ANNE.   Listen, in my heart
I love you for the partner you shall be,
But now, my dear, I ask you trust in me.
WILLIAM. Yet -
ANNE.   What?
WILLIAM.   I -
ANNE.   Hey!
WILLIAM.   Look -
ANNE.   Hmm?
WILLIAM.   Can't -
ANNE.   Please!
WILLIAM.   You -
ANNE.   No!
40   WILLIAM. Still -

ANNE.   Yes?
WILLIAM.   I -
ANNE.   Why?
WILLIAM.   We -
ANNE.   Lord!
WILLIAM.   I'm -
ANNE.   O!
WILLIAM.   Just -
ANNE.   Go!

Deflated, William drops his head.
Reflated, he raises an arm to Anne to say goodbye.
Anne blows him a kiss.
William catches it and puts it to his lips.
Exit William. Exit Anne, above.

Enter Audrey, Faith and Latimer.

AUDREY. We now be well within the danger grounds;
Tread carefully, and make no sudden sounds!
LATIMER. But what say we unto the guards that rein
Your cousin, Anne, behind her window pane?
FAITH. Were you not at rehearsals? Check the ink!
We ladies will seduce and spike their drink,
Then you shall swap your clothing with young Anne:
As you to girl, so she'll become a man!
AUDREY. I pray thee, hush! Let's hasten to her door,
50   Before Lord Edmund turns his daughter whore!

Exeunt.

III.4   *Enter Priest. He sings his own choral entrance music.*
PRIEST. I am the priest – you know that from my dress,
I have a little secret, I'll confess:
No, not the thing you're thinking - but that's true!
It's something that we givers like to do:
I spend my nights with medicines and herbs,
Creating brews; a potion that disturbs,
Or pleasures much the victim – volunteer!
Who taketh what we maketh. O, look here!
A tonic I made earlier this week,
10   It renders he that takes it soft and meek.
Quite often he can sleep as if he's dead,
And I can do whatever's in my head.
I let myself be ripe when nature calls:
I'm out! So he can -
Enter William.
WILLIAM.   Father!

PRIEST. *(surprised)*   LICK MY BALLS!
I pray, can you not learn to knock, my boy?
WILLIAM. What's in your hand?
PRIEST.   O, nothing! Just a toy!
What brings you here so early - where is Anne?
WILLIAM. She sent me back - she says she has a plan!
PRIEST. But I was told that Edmund -
WILLIAM.   So was I!
20   PRIEST. It seems she doth reality deny.
(Aside) As I'm a priest, I know this state too well,
That's why I'm using lubricants and gel:
I think of them as God's angelic hue,
That sanctify the naughty things I do!
(To William) Here, taketh thee this potion that I made;
Persuade her drink, so sleeping you may aid
By quietly removing her to here -
Once married ye have nothing more to fear!
WILLIAM. O Father, thou art such a quirky friend;
30   Your exploits will be spoke of at your end!
PRIEST. *(Aside)* I hope not! But, let's focus now on you:
Go save your girl!
WILLIAM.   I'll rescue!

                                    Exit William.

PRIEST.   Toodaloo!
I'm off to make more potions for my store;
I've twenty Williams, but I want more!
         Priest sings choral music.   *Exit Priest, singing.*
IV.1   *Enter Anne.*
ANNE. To be a girl is difficult, my friend:
It's hard to be respected and contend
With menfolk always targeting your wares;
There is no end to what libido dares!
Our lust to bed each other is so great,
That we will dive into a dire straight,
When all we crave is validation true:
Confirm that we are beautiful to you!
I know some ladies squander this, no doubt,
10   And disappear as soon as men reach out:
They do not do the brand of woman well,
As much as those with choices choose to sell.
Of course, we too are amorous and crave
The pleasure of a dark, dishonest knave,
But lie to us in parcels, not at once;

The light should slowly wax into the sconce!
We understand your situation now:
If milk is free, what need to buy the cow?
But if you would have children, then you must,
20   Consider deeper amity and trust.
So take your time and find an honest heart:
Our offspring all deserve a happy start.
Enter Audrey, Faith and Latimer.
AUDREY. I quite agree!
ANNE.   Why, Audrey, Faith and friend;
My sense another intrigue doth portend!
FAITH. To rescue you, we have a cunning plan;
O thank the stars we have this lovely man!
ANNE. But I am saved by Sidney's cool device.
LATIMER. You mean, Lord Edmund's servant?
FAITH.   He's not nice.
AUDREY. His reputation goes before his name.
30   FAITH. You cannot think that he won't cheat this game?
ANNE. I swear he's one of us!
AUDREY.   What evidence?
ANNE. He said his role was just one big pretence:
That he was waiting, sweet revenge to take,
Abiding for Lord Edmund's last mistake.
LATIMER. You're sure that you can trust him?
ANNE.   I think so.
FAITH. You cannot risk your life!
AUDREY.   Anne – we must go!
ANNE. O, very well then, tell me what to do?
      Latimer starts disrobing
LATIMER. Take off your clothes and I'll give mine to you!
ANNE. I beg your pardon?
FAITH.   Annie, don't be coy!
40   ANNE. *(disrobing)* My on-stage reputation you'll destroy!
EDMUND *(off)* O Anne, my sweet, my daughter new and fine,
I wonder, should you like to come and dine?
My servant did suggest I softly speak,
Perchance that I could later wet my beak?
O wait, did I just say that line out loud?
I'll start again – have dinner: don't be proud!
Or if you are not hungry, could we chat?
I wrote a poem, and I bought a cat!
     A cat meows off-stage.
ANNE. What should I say?

FAITH.   Say something!
AUDREY.   Use your wit!
50   ANNE. *(To Edmund)* Come woo me at my balcony!
LATIMER. *(In a very low, masculine voice)*   O shit!
I can't believe you did that – are you mad?
AUDREY. His acting isn't that good!
FAITH.   It's not bad!
LATIMER. I do not have your attributes; your bits!
I have the rump, but I don't have your -
AUDREY. *(Looking off)*   Tits!
I saw a blue tit at your window ledge!
                    Faith is dressing Latimer.
FAITH. We should have trimmed your eyebrows – that's a hedge!
ANNE. Then here I ask that you repair the seams:
You must become the girl Lord Edmund dreams!
                    Exit all but Faith and Latimer.
FAITH. I know that you can do it – best of luck!
60   But obviously, don't let his Lordship -
LATIMER.   Suck
Upon my lips for one more precious kiss:
For thee I'll be a lady – aye, a Miss!
                    Faith kisses Latimer.
                              Exit Faith.
A woman is seductive; soft and smooth:
A sexy actress, I – now watch me groove!
                    Exit Latimer, gracefully.
IV.2   *Enter Lord Edmund stroking a stuffed cat.*
EDMUND. At last my girl regained her senses true,
Hath lowered her defences to renew
Our loving words of family and trust;
I hope that she will remedy my lust!
Just like this little pussy in my hand,
I pray she purrs and rubs her anal gland
Against my palms of pleasure – kitty stop!
Don't bite or scratch; and please don't do a plop!
            The cat attacks Edmund. A struggle. Edmund kills it.
            He tosses it off-stage. He takes out a paper.
As customary in this fashion's fit,
10   I had a sonnet by a poet writ,
That I shall use to woo her from the slums,
Into my king-size bed! O look – she comes!
*Enter Latimer disguised as Anne, above. Per Act 3, scene 3 - if there is no
balcony available: Latimer enters holding Anne's 'balcony' block.*

Latimer steps on the block.
Lord Edmund slowly kneels to counter Latimer's lack of
balcony height.
O Anne, my little cauliflower green,
Can you forgive your papa? I was mean!
Latimer adopts a falsetto voice.
LATIMER. O sweet my lovely, gentle, sexy Lord,
Who is by me so suddenly adored!
I could forgive thy crime if thou might give
A sign of love, so happy I might live?
EDMUND. Ay yes, of course! No problem that for me,
For *I* have penned a sonnet for thee – see?
He shows her the paper.
LATIMER. O my!
EDMUND.   I shall poetically recite!
LATIMER. I'll cry!
EDMUND.   Now let me see – let's get this right:
Edmund reads from the paper.
"When I was just a teeny tiny boy,
I had a very teeny tiny toy,
I hoped that it would grow, but it did not:
Perhaps that's why I'm such a nasty clot?
Then I was older, son to noble man,
As ruler I was able thus to ban-
-ish peasants from my father's great estate!
But father left and mother did me hate!
So now I come, abegging on my knee,
And hope that you might laugh at what I plea:
Forgive this old and stupid, ugly fool,
Whom, if he could, would break you with his tool!
But even if it works, as I do preach,
Your special naughty parts he could not reach!"
Edmund crushes the paper.
I'll kill that bard!
LATIMER.   O what a pretty verse!
Such passion and such truth! Did you rehearse?
You've made me like you now!
EDMUND.   He has – have I?
LATIMER. Believe it, sir, my longing fills the sky!
EDMUND. *(Aside)* I should have been a poet – they get laid!
(To Latimer) I'll come straight up – I shall not be delayed!
LAT. *(bass voice)* What! No!
                    (falsetto) I mean, not yet, my Lord. Just wait!

20
30
40

Mechanically we're challenged! *(aside, bass)* - and I'm straight!
(falsetto) So let me to my bed – alone! To sleep:
Tomorrow we shall make our pleasure deep!
EDMUND. Of course, my pretty girl. Sleep well above,
And soon I'll shove my hand right up your glove!
LATIMER. O my!

Exit Latimer above.

Enter William, unseen by Lord Edmund.
        EDMUND.   Her change of heart brings change of face:
50   She has more beauty to her, and more grace;
Indeed she seems more shapely – more my type;
She is the fruit I'm craving - I am ripe!
So till this time tomorrow, too long hence,
I'll muse upon her burrow and it's fence!
Her bosom too – O! Whoops! I can't abstain!
I'll have to change my trousers, yet again!

Exit Edmund.

(off) O Sidney! Help me! Can you come and aid?
You won't believe the sticky mess I've made!
SIDNEY. *(off)* O God! That's what – three times today? No more!
EDMUND. *(off)* Don't wipe that bit!
SIDNEY. *(off)*   What this?
60   EDMUND. *(off)*   O No!
SIDNEY. *(off)*   THAT'S FOUR!
Slight pause.
        WILLIAM. He thinks on parts that he shall never play!
For I shall not allow my love to stay
To be the hankie to his Lordship's load:
Myself, I am about to full explode
With sheer delight, if I can have Anne sup
This potion, so to rest will go my pup!
I'll stroke her ample bosom and her hair,
Until she falls asleep, and then I'll dare
To carry her away unto the priest:
70   To marry us - our pleasure zones increased!
So let me call her now, from out her room:
I long to touch her panties, and her womb!
My Love! O sweet my Lady? It is I!
Approach your balcony! Just come say hi!
Enter Latimer dressed as Anne, above.
        LATIMER. Why, William?
WILLIAM.   O Anne?
LATIMER.   Is that my spouse?

William sees Latimer.
WILLIAM. WHAT DEVIL'S SPAWN!?
           (Aside) This cannot be her house!
Latimer adopts a falsetto voice.
LATIMER. I'm Anne!
WILLIAM.   My sweet, what happened to your face?
LATIMER. It's puffy – I was fighting with his Grace!
WILLIAM. Thy tender voice grew husky, did it not?
80   LATIMER. My screaming at Lord Edmund caused a knot:
A nodule on my larynx – it will pass;
Come up, so you can squeeze my juicy arse!
WILLIAM. So hot in passion, love – is ought amiss?
LATIMER. O William! I need a sloppy kiss!
WILLIAM. In sooth, I can't see well in this dull light,
But I shall climb for thee with all of my might.
LATIMER. O climb, love! Climb! And take me in thine arm!
WILLIAM. I come! I come! Yet drink thee first this charm.
LATIMER. What be its purpose?
WILLIAM.   It will help you sleep.
90   LATIMER. I'll put it by my bed.
WILLIAM.   Nay, drink it deep!
               Exit Latimer above.
(Aside) She does not look so well!
Enter Latimer above.
LATIMER.   How now, my pet!
O William! You haven't kissed me yet!
    They kiss, passionately.
WILLIAM. Thou hast a strange and yet familiar taste!
LATIMER. O ravish me, my love, our time don't waste!
    They kiss, passionately.
WILLIAM. Thy face is awfully scratchy; I've a rash!
LATIMER. I'm not a natural blonde – I shave my 'tash!
    They kiss. Latimer's wig comes off.
WILLIAM. Why, Latimer! What devil on God's earth?
Bethinkest thou that this is fitting mirth?
LATIMER. 'Tis so, my boy! A top and bottom jest:
100   You know you want to – squeeze my milky chest!
    Latimer kisses William.
WILLIAM. Get off! You raving idiot! Where's Anne?
LATIMER. We rescued her – she's with your holy man!
WILLIAM. O good companion! How I thee adore!
    William kisses Latimer, for slightly too long.
               Exit William.

LATIMER. *(Aside)* I wonder, could I? Should I? I'm not sure!
Exit Latimer above.

IV.3   *Enter Priest. He sings his own choral entrance music.*
PRIEST. Now William will be about his deed,
For he is swift in passion, yes indeed;
We've had our special moments, he and I,
He's kept me ridged, that I can't deny!
He's beat me of-ten: much to my delight,
When we played naked twister, half the night.
He is to games, as poetry to Bard:
I tell him plain -
Enter Anne dressed in Latimer's attire.
ANNE.   O Father!
PRIEST. *(surprised)*   SUCKETH HARD!
Did you not see the sign upon my tree?
10   I'm musing on my sermon!
ANNE.   So I see!
Is something poking, underneath your dress?
PRIEST. I'm sorry, did you come here to confess?
ANNE. O no, I came to marry me a man!
PRIEST. O good! You're one of us!
ANNE.   My name is Anne!
PRIEST. I'm sometimes, Betty – pleased to meet you, dear.
ANNE. I think there's been a mix-up happened here.
PRIEST. That's what I said, a chromosome or two;
But now, my man, bend over – say I do!
ANNE. Excuse me? O, you think that I'm a bloke?
20   Let me remove my clothes!
Anne takes off Latimer's clothes.
PRIEST. *(aside)*   Let's have a poke!
O wait! You are a woman!
ANNE.   Yes, I'm Anne!
PRIEST. You're here for William?
ANNE.   That was the plan!
Enter Audrey and Faith.
AUDREY. I see the bride of William you know:
Did you just look, or did you have a go?
PRIEST. I'm not that way inclined, you silly tart!
AUDREY. I warn you, Priest – there's anger in my heart!
FAITH. Why Audrey! Do you doubt our cousin's trust?
AUDREY. I don't! It's just this play is full of lust!
I meant no slur unto our noble kin,
30   But Priest, a grope or fondle is a sin!

ANNE. Believe me, Audrey, nothing is amiss,
But that, as I was man, he did dismiss
My claims to William, so I undressed!
PRIEST. For once that is the truth, I can attest!
AUDREY. Ah, well, forgive me; now I understand!
FAITH. Let's have a wedding! Someone start the band!
PRIEST. But William is elsewhere!
FAITH. *(aside)*   O my God!
PRIEST. I sent him back to yours.
AUDREY.   You stupid sod!
ANNE. Then I must go, to meet him at his quest:

40   As Fathers go, I don't think you're the best!
> *Exit Anne.*

FAITH. I must agree!
AUDREY.   Your conduct doth appal!
FAITH. We're talking to the press!
AUDREY.   We're telling all!
> *Exit Audrey and Faith.*

PRIEST. Perhaps it's best I grant a self-reprieve:
It's time to pack my toys; some boys – and leave!
> *Priest sings choral music. Exit Priest, quickly, singing.*

IV.4   *Enter Latimer, dressed as Anne.*

LATIMER. So I abide within Anne's chamber here,
Her silky garments pressing to me near,
I'm comfortable; I'm happy as can be:
So nice for all my tackle to swing free!
And thus should Edmund breach into her room,
Within the darkness he might be my groom!
I wouldn't let him go that far, of course;
I'd want that Sidney – what a hobbyhorse!
But I might serve to Edmund keep at bay,

10   So Anne and William can get away.
But soft! Who is't comes hither to surprise?
I must retake my feminine disguise!

Enter Sidney.

SIDNEY. How now, fair Anne, I wanted to convey
That we have all we need to end this play!
LATIMER. O Sidney, that's terrific! What good news!
> *Latimer turns his back on Sidney and bends over.*

I want to show you – I can touch my shoes!
SIDNEY. That's very clever! Are you feeling well?
LATIMER. Perchance you take my temperature to tell?
The oldest method I perceive is best:

20   Within my cheeks, I urge you, come and rest!
SIDNEY. I beg your pardon, did I hear you right?
LATIMER. I do assure thee, sir, I'm super tight!
SIDNEY. It must be all the stress; this is not you!
LATIMER. I'm curious! Just do what menfolk do!
SIDNEY. Upon your father's honour, I could not!
LATIMER. O give it to me big boy – fill my slot!
SIDNEY. Well, maybe just a quick one – no, no, no!
LATIMER. I've been a naughty school girl – spank me so!
Pause.   *Sidney considers it. No.*
SIDNEY. I also came to warn thee: Edmund wakes;
30   I fear that he may come and up the stakes.
So mend thy mind, and put away thy butt;
Don't give a whiff of interest to that mutt!
        Latimer moves towards Sidney and seduces him.
LATIMER. Perhaps, then, just one kiss to calm my nerves?
I need your strength - it's what a girl deserves!
        Latimer kisses Sidney, passionately.
        He then poses, suggestively.
Now take me quick, be rough as you can be!
SIDNEY. I've got to go. It isn't you, it's me.
        Exit Sidney.
LATIMER. Of course, I knew he'd wouldn't all along!
(unconvincingly) I don't like men. It's naughty, weird, and wrong!
Enter Lord Edmund.
EDMUND. I see my joyful girl is yet awake,
40   And taller/smaller, somehow, is it my mistake,
Or do you tower/cower, here before mine eye?
LATIMER. O playful Lord! I'm tired, so goodbye!
EDMUND. Then let me help thee hence unto thy rest.
LATIMER. O no, my Lord! Go shoo! You randy pest!
EDMUND. Yet I insist!
LATIMER.   O stop it, Edmund, please!
EDMUND. I want you!
LATIMER.   Not tonight!
EDMUND.   You always tease!
Pause.

LATIMER. O very well, then! Just the smallest kiss!
EDMUND. Then close thine eyes so I can sample bliss!
        They kiss.
LATIMER. Well, honestly, my Lord. That wasn't bad!
EDMUND. I see you want another?
50   LATIMER.   Drive me mad!

They kiss. Latimer's wig falls off.
EDMUND. O wait a minute! Goodness! You're a man!
Thou filthy base impostor! Where is Anne?
You do not wish to tell me? We shall see:
I've quite the night of games in store for thee!
(shouts off) O Sidney!
Enter Sidney.
    SIDNEY.   Yes, sir!
    EDMUND.   Look, a cunning ploy:
My Anne is switched for this – this lady-boy!
        Sidney reacts: retching and spitting, etc.
Good lord, man. What's this business? Are you ill?
SIDNEY. 'Tis just the shock, my Lord. *(Aside)* A bitter pill!
EDMUND. Go chain him to my dirty dungeon knob;
60   I'll school him – from behind – and call him, 'Bob'!
        Exeunt Edmund, then Sidney with Latimer.
IV.5   *Enter William, singing choral music.*
WILLIAM. O Father! Priest! It's William, your boy;
I heard from Latimer about their ploy!
The night hath waxed a pace, could he to bed?
Yet where is Anne? Am I here in her stead?
Enter Priest with luggage.
PRIEST. O William, my son. You're back alone?
What happened? Did the wedding Anne postpone?
WILLIAM. My friend just sent me here to meet my *frau*!
PRIEST. Anne came and stood where you are standing now.
On hearing you were missing, she was vexed!
10   She headed home.
WILLIAM. *(checks his phone)* I should have sent a text.
        The priest opens his luggage. Checks a few things.
PRIEST. I hope that all works out, but I must flea:
The media and law are on to me!
        William joins the priest and looks in his luggage.
WILLIAM. But where is it you're going in such haste?
That's quite a trunk! Are you being replaced?
        William finds, and holds up, a large sex toy - he is
        confused and unsure of what it is.
PRIEST. Unto the Vatican I'm being flown:
        Priest grabs and shoves the toy back in his bag.
The Diocese, thank God, protects their own!
About our little secret – hold it tight.
        Priest shuts his bag.
WILLIAM. Your face will haunt me, every single night!

Sirens are heard. Priest grabs his bag and runs.
PRIEST. O fudge! Five O! I'll have to take my van!
Exit Priest.

20   WILLIAM. *(Aside)* Now how to bring the spotlight back to Anne?
I'll have a missive envoyed to my dear:
Using his phone
"Am back at church. In basement. Meet me here."
I'm off now, to the basement. Like I said.
I'm tired. See me yawning? Time for bed.
Exit William.

IV.6   *Enter Sidney, drinking.*
SIDNEY. The night hath been a strange one, that's for sure;
I cannot quite believe you stayed for more!
Yet, all considered: elements of plot;
Theatrical devices; masks; the lot!
The lovers sweet; the predators; the ball,
The sexual innuendo – O the gall!
The architect of all these scenes - the cuts:
This man is either genius, or nuts!
How does he get away with it, I ask?
10   Within a rhyming spotlight he doth bask!
Could it be true – has Shakespeare come alive?
Did Molière learn English and survive?
Whatever be the truth, I'll tell ye this:
The clergy might give rhyming verse a miss!
Enter Anne, still in her underwear, with Audrey and Faith.
ANNE. O Sidney! Can I trust you? What has passed?
Is William, my boyfriend here at last?
I met a sketchy priest; I got undressed:
O tell me is he here? I'm getting stressed!
SIDNEY. I know not where thy lover is, dear Anne,
20   But Edmund's in his dungeon with a man.
The screaming groans of pleasure long begun;
Whatever goes, I think they're having fun!
ANNE. O William! Wherefore are we ill-met?
EDMUND. *(off)* Whoever's out there shouting will regret!
Enter Edmund.
O look! My newfound daughter hath returned,
With all her friends, together they have yearned
To join me in the dungeon for the night:
I've got the hots for all of you – that's right!
My Sidney!
SIDNEY.   Yes, sir!

EDMUND.   Take them down below,
30   Then lock Anne in her chamber!
SIDNEY.   Off you go!
Exeunt all but Edmund.
EDMUND. Now with this final couplet of the scene,
I'll give an evil laugh to show I'm mean!
Ha-ha-ha-ha-ha-ha-ha-ha-ha-har!
Ha-ha-ha-ha-ha-ha-ha-ha-ha-har!
Exit Edmund.

Enter Chorus.
> CHORUS. So, William doth languish in his plan,
> The Priest is off to Rome in creepy van,
> Whilst Audrey, dainty Latimer and Faith
> Are in Lord Edmund's dungeon – locked up safe.
> He's working on them slowly, one by one,
> The things he does I dare not speak upon!
> You've all seen that Pulp Fiction film, I'm sure?
> We have a gimp and lubricants galore!
> I'll let imagination take the reins:

10   What pleasures some can cause the other pains!
> But less about the clergy, to the plot,
> Let's separate what is and what is not:
> For Anne, within her chamber found a drug;
> She drank and fell asleep upon her rug.
> > > > *Exit Chorus.*

V.1   *Enter Edmund and Sidney.*
      EDMUND. Good-morrow, Sidney – what a night I passed!
      So peaceful in my slumber! How's the cast?
      I know I gave them quite a shock last night:
      Pray tell, coadjutant, are they all right?
      SIDNEY. Here are the notes, as best I can deduct:
      Since Anne is still asleep, I did instruct
      That Latimer, the one still in a frock,
      With Faith and Audrey, 'pon her door do knock,
      So they may preen and primp her for your view:
A loud cry offstage.
10   EDMUND. Good heavens! What was that – is much ado?
Enter Audrey. She is very angry, insulting and bitter. This speech should be played as if the actress playing Audrey is deliberately hijacking the scene - using 'her big moment' on-stage to rant to the audience about the author (who is in the audience) not allowing her to play the leading role of Anne. Occasionally she uses some of the lines she was supposed to deliver from the play, but mainly it's a very loud, and large, seemingly improvised, attack on the playwright - her ex-lover. The rest of the cast should be stunned - as if the actress is having a total meltdown, completely destroying the scene/play - and there's nothing they can do about it until she's done. Audrey should imagine the writer in a specified place in the audience, and direct most of her angst to that seat, as she attempts to turn the rest of the audience against the writer for his, alleged, wrongdoings against her.
      AUDREY. Since I, ostensibly, could not play Anne,
      And "wasn't right for Faith", so said the man,
      The writer gave me here a heavy speech:
      Apparently I'm Audrey – I can preach!
      I'm told, "it's not my time" to play the lead,
      Despite that with the author I did plead,
      Upon my knees – within his bedroom, late:
            She squeezes her breasts.
      I showed him all my goods – he took them straight!
      But that did nothing to secure the part:
20   He's overly protective of his 'art'!
      (Mocking) And so, it falls to 'Audrey', here to tell,
      How Anne, our 'on-stage beauty', is in hell!
            Suddenly and dramatically.
      (To Edmund) You've murdered love and hope!
                      (to the writer) A bulky line!
      (To Edmund) Thou devil! O, what ignorant design!
      (Aside) My cousin, Anne, is not asleep – no way!
      She took an overdose – she's gone away!

Departed from this life – *(directed off)* BRING IN THE STIFF!
Enter Latimer and Faith (in shock) bearing Anne's body.
Behold her sacred body – take a whiff!
    She wafts her hand to her nose, breathing in.
She's now a rotting carcass – want a kiss?
30   SIDNEY. O god!
AUDREY.   Your interjections I dismiss!
I've started so I'll finish, as they say:
    She really starts to lose it now. She is very loud and
    completely unhinged until the end.
I DON'T KNOW WHAT I'M DOING IN THIS PLAY!
I run around expressing odd lines here,
But do I have a through-line? It's not clear!
It's obvious that Faith is just the slut!
    All gasp.
And Anne, she has the writer's favourite butt!
    All gasp. Anne looks up at Audrey in disgust, before
    remembering to be dead.
Yet who is Audrey – how can I play true?
The audience don't have a bloody clue!
O yes, I know – get back into the scene:
40   *(insincerely)* O Edmund, you're a villain! You are mean!
Ok, I'll stop my ranting – back to work;
(loud, at the writer) It's not my fault the writer is a jerk!
    She's finally back on script.
(sincerely, acting well) O horror! Horror! Look, thou vile man:
You've murdered my sweet cousin! O poor Anne!
    Audrey sobs over Anne's body.
EDMUND. *(Timidly)* You're finished?
AUDREY. *(Violently, at Edmund)*   Yes! I'm finished!
EDMUND. *(over-dramatically)*   Anne is broke!
Now I must strive to bear this heavy yoke!
Enter William.
WILLIAM. O desperate vision! O what sight is this?
    Approaching and wooing a grateful Audrey.
Important actress, I would ask but this:
    Audrey and William are millimetres away from kissing.
That I impart unto thy cousin's lips
50   A kiss – I'll skip the breast and leave the hips,
And marry her in death as I would life.
    William reaches into his pants.
I might just join her – look, I brought a knife!
    William pulls out a dagger.

It's big and shiny!
AUDREY. *(admiring his dagger)* Oh, my god! That's nice!
You'd penetrate my flesh with your device!
So take thy nuptial kiss from our good Anne:
She cannot move. She needs her leading man!
WILLIAM. I thank thee, Madame, for thy most kind wish.
They almost kiss.
William suddenly turns away and focuses on Anne.
For ages now my tongue hath sought this dish;
Throughout rehearsals, from the first read-through:

60   I dare not speak the things I long to do!
I must say, our director does cast well:
I'd follow her to heaven, or to hell!
He kisses Anne, slowly.
Mmmmm. That was nice. I may just drag this out;
Another kiss – in character, no doubt.
He kisses Anne, slowly.
Mmmmm. Yes! I have a pretty awesome job!
My girlfriend's even watching as my gob
Delights itself upon this hot girl's face.
Now what's my line? O crap! I've lost my place!
I have it! Yes! To unity – rebirth!
Holding the dagger to his chest.

70   For there is nothing for me on this earth!
Anne wakes.
ANNE. O William!
WILLIAM. *(surprised)* O Anne! Am I asleep?
ANNE. No, that was me – I drank that potion deep!
WILLIAM. O look what acting's fortune hath me brung:
Another kiss! *(aside)* For sure, I'll slip the tongue!
William sticks out his tongue and moves towards Anne.
Edmund comes forth.
EDMUND. If she's alive the next kiss will be mine!
WILLIAM. I do not want to share her – she's divine!
EDMUND. I tell thee she's my daughter, not your wife!
SIDNEY. Excuse me, matey – can I use your knife?
William gives Sidney his dagger. Sidney stabs Edmund.
EDMUND. O Sidney! Why? You traitor! O my rage!

80   SIDNEY. Come with me, sir – 'tis best to kill offstage.
Exit Sidney with Edmund.
EDMUND. *(off)* No, Sidney! Take your hands off me, you swine!
Please wait! I'll give you money!
SIDNEY. *(off)*   I resign!

FAITH. What's going on?

AUDREY. He's stabbing him some more.

FAITH. Lord Edmund's fighting back!

AUDREY. He's on the floor!

LATIMER. *(aside)* O gosh!

FAITH. That Sidney knows a move or two!

AUDREY. He's kicking arse!

FAITH. I heard he does Kung-Fu!

LATIMER. *(aside)* Bad Sidney!

EDMUND. *(off)* Oooo!

FAITH. That's quite a nasty note!

AUDREY. Lord Edmund's done.

FAITH. That Sidney slit his throat!

Enter Sidney, bloodied. Everyone claps, politely.

SIDNEY. I did us all a favour; there's no doubt:

90   For years I had been musing on that bout!

And look ye, here's a legal paper plea

That states that Anne is heir to all you see!

Enter Magistrate.

The magistrate, who just by chance, arrived

Will now confirm the intrigue thus contrived.

MAGISTRATE. O yes, it's true. The case is strong and sound:

Anne gets it all – the castle and the ground;

The full estate is hers!

ANNE. What of his wife?

MAGISTRATE. Can Sidney think of something?

SIDNEY. Where's that knife?

WILLIAM. O Anne, can you believe it? We are rich!

100   ANNE. What's all this "we" talk, buster? You're my bitch!

Anne dominates William as they kiss. All cheer.

SIDNEY. We'll meet you in the bar for our review!

WILLIAM. Till then, farewell.

ANNE. Till then, sweet love, adieu.

Exeunt.

EPILOGUE

Enter Chorus.
  CHORUS. So now our scene hath ended – thank the Lord!
  With everything resolved in sweet accord,
  It's time to ponder on its themes and plot:
  The way we live our lives before we rot.
  What did we learn? What will you talk about?
    He points to 'faucet lady' in the front row.
  What dirty little secrets will come out?
  Consider, as you leave this place tonight
  Those destitute, poor creatures of the night.
  I speak, of course, of actors – much like me,
10 Please tell the world of what ye here did see:
  Your kind review upon our rhyming feat
  Will help this troupe of starving actors eat!
  We thus entreat ye, kindle kindness now:
  Let proud applause attend our humble bow.
         He bows and exits.

ABOUT THE AUTHOR

Ryan J-W Smith, BA Theatre Studies, MA Law (*Dist*), is primarily: a critically acclaimed poet; a multi award-winning verse playwright; a critically acclaimed actor/director/producer; a festival-winning filmmaker; a composer and musician; a legal scholar; and, a successful business entrepreneur working professionally in the entertainment industry for around thirty years.

From the age of five until fifteen, Smith trained to be a professional tennis player – beating Britain's future Men's Number 1 in straight sets at the age of thirteen. Wimbledon was in his sights… Injury at the age of fifteen may have subsequently set him on a different path, but Ryan never lost the champion's mindset: one of vision, dedication, positivity, iron-clad resilience and, above all else, an extraordinary work ethic.

Receiving a full scholarship from the European Union, Smith read Theatre Studies at Trinity College, Dublin. During his studies he was also awarded a scholarship from Trinity as the highest achieving student in his year.

After Trinity, Ryan quickly evolved to become a multi award-winning verse playwright/director/producer/actor via his own theatre company, Rogue Shakespeare®. His artistic accolades in this area include: two-time Hollywood Fringe International Award Winner (and four-time nominee); two-time Encore Producers' Award Winner; Hollywood Fringe Comedy Award Nomination; Amnesty International Freedom of Expression Award Nomination; Gandhi Foundation Award Recipient; three-time Arts Council England Award Recipient, and countless professional 4 and 5-star reviews.

Having now written over 2,000 Shakespearean sonnets, along with 7 verse plays, Smith has firmly established himself as a uniquely dedicated and internationally critically-acclaimed award-winning poet.

Ryan is also a musician (primarily playing the guitar and piano) and a composer. His first two solo albums were originally released with Universal Music.

Ryan is also a festival-winning filmmaker. His films have been shown, selected for, nominated or won their categories at over 25 international film festivals, including Cannes.

Smith graduated from law school with a Master's Degree in Law, awarded with distinction. He has a particular focus and interest in Medical Law and Ethics; Contract Law; EU Law, and Criminal Law. Smith is a very strong advocate of civil liberties, freedom of speech and bodily autonomy.

Ryan is a long-time practitioner of the Buddhist arts of Mindfulness Meditation and Wing Chun Kung-Fu. Smith considers Buddhist philosophy to be the foundation of all of his achievements and skills.

Smith is also the founder and senior agent of the internationally renowned British Talent Agency®.

ROGUE
SHAKESPEARE®

The award-winning cast of Smith's Love Labours Won, Hollywood, 2015.

www.rogueshakespeare.com

Also available by

RYAN J-W SMITH

Sweet Love Adieu (original version)
ISBN-13: 978-0-9515956-2-6   EAN: 9780951595626
First published in 2003, Duckpaddle Publishing Ltd.

The Power Play
ISBN-13: 978-0-9515956-3-3   EAN: 9780951595633
First published in 2003, Duckpaddle Publishing Ltd.

Scan the QR codes or order via:

www.rogueshakespeare.com

www.ryanjwsmith.com

RYAN J-W SMITH

500 SHAKESPEAREAN SONNETS

The Diary of a Poetic Quest for Truth

"Candid, spiritual, philosophical and sometimes boldly political...
a landmark in literature"
Watkins Magazine

"Shakespeare managed to write 154 - Smith has penned more than three
times that number. ...splendidly contemporary... a tour de force"
Herald Scotland

"Impressively well-constructed... often startlingly expressive and insightful...
a fascinating and richly detailed picture of the author"
Neon Literary Magazine

"Shakespeare's record of 154 sonnets in his lifetime was breathtaking.
But what Ryan J-W Smith has achieved is simply awe-inspiring. Thought-
provoking, political, even hard-hitting at times, this collection of sonnets,
which took 4 years to write, is honest and very real. There is no layer to
scrape through - the reader is honoured with a very truthful portrayal of life,
which is beautifully crafted. Highly recommended"
Book A Poet

"Like reading someone's diary, their private thoughts and feelings captured
in verse... this collection shows a tremendous talent, and deserves to sit along
side your Poes, Plaths, and T.S Elliots."
Mass Movement Magazine

"Incredibly well written... a poetic achievement. A great gift for any
poetry lover in your life. Stunning stuff."
Frost Magazine

"An honest process of learning, healing and repentance...
a collection of inspirational, honest and didactic poetry"
Mouth London

"Masters of the Verse - Smith pays homage to the Bard with the
must-read collection of his own modern verse"
London Planner